NATURAL LAW
and
PUBLIC REASON

NATURAL LAW
and
PUBLIC REASON

edited by

Robert P. George
Christopher Wolfe

GEORGETOWN UNIVERSITY PRESS / WASHINGTON, D.C.

Georgetown University Press, Washington, D.C.
©2000 by Georgetown University Press. All rights reserved.
Printed in the United States of America

10 9 8 7 6 5 4 3 2 1   2000

This volume is printed on acid-free offset book paper.

Library of Congress Cataloging-in-Publication Data

Natural law and public reason / edited by Robert P. George,
   Christopher Wolfe.
     p. cm.
   Includes index.
   ISBN 0-87840-765-0 (cloth : alk. paper). — ISBN 0-87840-766-9
(paper : alk. paper)
    1. Natural law. 2. Liberalism. 3. Reason. 4. Rawls, John, 1921–
—Contributions in political science. I. George, Robert P.
II. Wolfe, Christopher.
K460.N349 2000
340'.112—dc21   99-38853
                                                               CIP

Contents

Robert P. George and Christopher Wolfe

Introduction

As the century winds to a close, John Rawls remains a—perhaps the—central figure in Anglo-American political philosophy. In his 1993 book, *Political Liberalism*,[1] Rawls reformulated, and in certain respects revised, the liberal theory of political morality he advanced in *A Theory of Justice* (1971).[2] Still, the upshot of Rawls's theory is the same: when it comes to "constitutional essentials and matters of basic justice," political power may not be exercised on the basis of controversial judgments of what makes for, or detracts from, a valuable and morally worthy way of life.

A key concept that Rawls has introduced in support of the "political liberalism" he espouses is the idea of "public reason."[3] The Rawlsian doctrine of public reason provides a new form of justification for the "bracketing" of fundamental and controversial moral, philosophical, and religious issues in politics—largely removing these issues from the agenda of political life in liberal democratic societies. Nonliberals, or at least those whose liberalism is of an older and more traditional stripe—especially those whose fundamental views are shaped by religion or ideas about natural law—are naturally suspicious of such a doctrine. Public reason is a doctrine devised and promoted by Rawls and other liberals—indeed, by people whose liberalism is not merely "political," in Rawls's terms, but also "comprehensive"—and it almost always has the effect of making the liberal position the winner in morally charged political controversies. It does this, in effect, by ruling out of bounds substantive moral argument on behalf of nonliberal positions.[4]

Proponents of natural law doctrines can go in two somewhat different directions regarding the idea of public reason, depending on how that idea is understood. On the one hand, if "public reason" is interpreted broadly (perhaps we could even say literally), then natural law theorists believe that natural law theory is nothing more or less than the philosophy of public reason. Acting according to right reason—for good reasons—is, after all, precisely what natural law is all about. Those who promote natural law doctrines believe that their views are based on "political values everyone can reasonably be expected to endorse"—again, taking "political" and "reasonably" in their normal, broad senses.

On the other hand, if "public reason" is interpreted in the narrower sense in which Rawls uses the phrase—a sense in which public reason generally excludes reliance on "comprehensive" moral, philosophical, and religious doctrines—then natural law theorists reject the idea, precisely because it attempts to put the grounds, and often the substance, of people's deepest moral convictions off-limits in the most important public discourse. The Rawlsian doctrine of public reason excludes a significant portion of what natural law theorists maintain can be known by reason—a portion which, from their point of view, is of the utmost relevance to basic questions of justice and the common good. So, according to natural law theorists, this truncated doctrine of public reason is itself unreasonable.

This volume is an effort to examine the doctrine of public reason. Stephen Macedo leads off by arguing that liberalism involves not only a substantive commitment to liberty and equality, but also a more procedural commitment to "public reasonableness." Liberals "seek political principles that can be publicly justified and widely affirmed by reasonable people in a diverse society." Public reason, especially as articulated by John Rawls, is a way to overcome the difficulties occasioned by deep differences among citizens in their comprehensive religious and philosophical views, by providing a "self-supporting" public morality.

Macedo elaborates the demands of public reason by examining its implications for two issues that have divided Americans: abortion and slavery. With respect to abortion, he argues that since people can reasonably disagree about this issue, "the best thing may be to try and give something to both sides, even if on balance one believes one side to be right and the other wrong." It is a failure of reasonableness, then, to say, as pro-life thinkers Robert George and John Finnis do, that abortion is "not even a close call." With respect to slavery, however, there is no room for reasonable disagreement. The most that can be said for pro-slavery arguments is that a certain respect is owed to persons who in general exhibit reasonableness and good will, but this does not require us to consider the pro-slavery position as publicly reasonable, since we can rightly regard it as so deeply misguided and wrong as to be unworthy of respect. Macedo concludes that public reasonableness should retain a central place in our political morality, for it holds out the possibility that people of fundamentally differing views might live together peacefully in a political community based on a form of reasonableness they can share.

Robert George and Christopher Wolfe respond by raising a series of questions about what liberal "public reason" means, especially with regard to the requirements that arguments be "publicly accessible" and "not too complex." They analyze and reject Macedo's contention that natural law theory necessarily entails judgments that do not meet these standards, arguing that there are forms of "inarticulate" but genuine human knowledge that are typically the basis of any judgments that are plausibly "publicly accessible." Does Macedo give us compelling reasons to think that arguments against slavery are truly "publicly accessible," whereas those against abortion are not (or are less so)? Even apart from what they contend is Macedo's misunderstanding of a key element of George's argument against abortion, they contend that Macedo fails to show that anti-slavery arguments can be regarded as meeting the test of public reason, while anti-abortion arguments do not. George and Wolfe conclude with a brief discussion of public reason and religion, indicating their serious doubts as to whether the liberal doctrine of public reason is any more helpful regarding those issues.

John Finnis, like George and Wolfe, expresses a willingness to accept the standard of "public reason," but only if it is understood, not in the Rawlsian sense, but in the wider sense that corresponds to important features of natural law theory. Finnis argues that Rawls himself is ambiguous as to whether his form of public reason is a predictive or normative concept. Moreover, according to Finnis, Rawls gives no reason to think that principles of justice chosen outside his "original position" are false. His case for the liberal "legitimacy principle" begs the important questions, and in fact that principle is itself illegitimate, unreasonable, and uncivil. In Finnis's view, Rawls's criterion of reciprocity seems fair, but applying it to the issue of abortion yields conclusions quite contrary to Rawls's own assertions, and to those of the U.S. Supreme Court, on that issue. No valid reason for tolerating the killing of unborn human beings, but not the killing of born ones, has been offered, either by the Court or by pro-choice philosophers. Finnis contends that Jeffrey Reiman's attempt to ground a difference in the "principle of subjective preference" exemplifies the failure of such efforts.

Professor Reiman, while agreeing with Finnis and others (against Rawlsian public reason) that the legality of abortion must be publicly determined, develops a variant reading of liberal public reason that provides a different defense of a right to abortion. Reiman's "comprehensive" liberalism aims to guarantee what he takes to be the necessary condition of a good life, namely, that it be "self-governed." So, Reiman contends, people should be allowed to formulate and act on their own judgments of how it is best to live (compatible with the like right of others to do so). According to this view, natural law certainly can have a place in public discussion, but it is incompatible with public reason, insofar as it attempts to provide the basis for coercing people on matters of how to live.

For example, the empirical intractability of differing judgments by intelligent people of good will regarding the status of the fetus would make the natural law proscription of abortion incompatible with public reason. The controversial position on the status of a fetus within a woman must give way to the uncontroversial right of a woman to control her body. Moreover, liberal discourse (Reiman's version of "public reason") must abide by the principles of subjective preference and individual priority, according to which (1) arguments about public coercion must be made in terms of what people want, not in terms of intrinsic worth, because intrinsic worth arguments risk imposing judgments about the best life on others, contrary to liberal principles, and (2) what a person wants or desires for herself has a very strong presumption over what any number of others want or desire for her.

In this context, Reiman appeals to the "asymmetric value of human life" to decide the abortion issue. Temporally symmetric value is the sort of value that gives us roughly equal reasons for not destroying existing valuable Xs and for creating new valuable Xs, and since destroying human lives and not creating them are morally very different, the value of human life must be asymmetrical. This rules out appeal to any notions of intrinsic human worth, since such notions would bestow value roughly equally on future humans and on existing ones. What accounts for the asymmetrical value of human life and provides a basis for respecting some human lives (but not the lives of fetuses) is that at some point, humans are aware of being who they are and care strongly about, or at least count strongly upon, their continuing to stay alive.

Paul Weithman examines Rawlsian public reason, asking particularly about how it applies to ordinary citizens engaging in political discussion and action. He argues that the requirements of Rawlsian public reason are best understood as role-specific duties of citizenship rather than as prima facie moral obligations. But he suggests that Rawls's conception of citizenship is not the most appropriate one for determining the role-specific duties of ordinary American citizens and that the requirements of public reason are not among those duties. Ordinary citizens may put forward a much wider array of arguments than Rawls's account of public reason permits (though public reason does impose some constraints).

In particular, liberal conceptions of justice do not rule out, as Rawls contends they do, appeal by citizens to their "comprehensive" views. According to Rawls, such appeals threaten the possibility that all will believe that constitutional essentials and matters of basic justice are settled consistent with the status of each person as a free and equal coholder of society's final political power, and also threaten the "fundamental political relation of citizenship" by undermining mutual trust and mutual respect. Weithman tries to show that this contention is wrong by appealing to the examples of Martin Luther King, Jr. and Abraham Heschel, who made such appeals to comprehensive views without undermining the requisite mutual trust and respect, and he offers an explanation of why this was possible. Moreover, he argues that Rawls's requirements are grounded in a conception of citizenship that is not appropriate for the United States.

Patrick Neal takes up questions about Rawlsian public reason from the perspective of what Rawls refers to as a "citizen of faith." Religious believers reject Rawls's account of liberal justice and public reason less because of the practical implications it might have than because it provides an unfair and distorted description of the religious challenge to public reason. This distortion is the source of the mistaken view that it would be unreasonable to reject what Rawls calls the "duty of civility," with its requirement of participation in public reason (as Rawls understands it) when making decisions about basic justice and constitutional essentials.

Rawls wants religious believers to be "wholehearted members of a democratic society who endorse society's intrinsic political ideals and values and do not simply acquiesce in the balance of political and social forces." What particularly bothers religious believers (even those who understand themselves to be committed to the political values of liberty and equality) is that Rawls characterizes the failure to subordinate their comprehensive views as selfish, self-interested action, when in fact it represents their view of what morality and justice require. Neal points out that Rawls's arguments in support of liberal public reason parallel the arguments in *A Theory of Justice* that treated religious beliefs as irrelevant from the standpoint of justice, such as race, sex, occupation, and wealth. Moreover, Rawls's discourse in *Political Liberalism* almost always proceeds against the background assumption of a society that to a substantial degree embodies widespread commitment to the fundamental principles of political liberalism, sparing him the need to confront a scenario in which the principles of justice regulating the political realm in a society would contradict the fundamental requirements of his own comprehensive moral view.

According to Neal, the refusal of citizens of faith to subordinate their comprehensive views to Rawlsian public reason should not be misinterpreted either as a selfish insistence on holding out for a better deal for one's personal interests, or as a refusal to show respect for one's fellow citizens as equals. In fact, he argues, to characterize the refusal to subordinate comprehensive views that way is itself a denial of equal respect to fellow citizens. Arguably, one displays respect for one's adversaries by simply stating clearly that one thinks their views are wrong, rather than by avoiding the question of truth and describing their views as publicly "unreasonable" (though, in theory, possibly true).

The doctrine of liberal public reason was intended by Rawls to make the contemporary liberal contractarian project more defensible. Critics contend that liberal public reason fails to accomplish this goal, resolving earlier problems only by creating a host of new but similarly intractable ones. At the same time, such critics may treat the debate over liberal public reason as pointing beyond liberalism to the development of a more adequate conception of public reason—one that is not arbitrarily curtailed or truncated.

This book is based on panels sponsored by the American Public Philosophy Institute (APPI) at the 1998 and 1999 American Political Science Association annual meetings. The APPI is a group of scholars, mostly working in the tradition of natural law ethics and jurisprudence, who view themselves as firmly committed to the ideal of public reason. This commitment is manifest in their promotion of the intellectual engagement of the natural law tradition with liberalism and other contemporary schools of moral and political theory. From this engagement they believe that much light can be shed on crucial issues facing our polity and society today.

Notes

1. John Rawls, *Political Liberalism*. New York: Columbia University Press, 1993.
2. John Rawls, *A Theory of Justice*. Cambridge, Mass.: The Belknap Press of Harvard University Press, 1971.
3. *Political Liberalism*, Lecture VI. See also Rawls, "The Idea of Public Reason Revisited," *University of Chicago Law Review* 64 (1997), 765.
4. In the first edition of *Political Liberalism* (p. 243, n. 32), for example, Rawls argued that, assuming three important political values—due respect for human life, the ordered reproduction of political society over time (including the family), and the equality of women as equal citizens—"any reasonable balance of these three values will give a woman a duly qualified right to decide whether or not to end her pregnancy during the first trimester." Rawls later seemed to retract this statement in "The Idea of Public Reason Revisited" (p. 798, nn. 80 and 82), at least leaving open the possibility of an argument in public reason denying the right to abortion. But this admission, even on an issue where natural law moral argu-

ments can most easily be framed in terms of a right fundamental in liberal theory (the right to life), only highlights the exclusion of comprehensive moral doctrines from public reason. So, for example, moral arguments regarding the status of homosexual acts seem to be excluded from the "political values" that will determine the question of "same-sex marriage." See "Public Reason Revisited," p. 788, n. 60.

Stephen Macedo

In Defense of Liberal Public Reason: Are Slavery and Abortion Hard Cases?

Introduction: Two-Part Liberalism

I want to defend a version of liberalism that is made up of two parts: on the one hand a commitment to broad guarantees of liberty and equality, on the other hand a commitment to a practice of public reasonableness. The first part is the most widely known and discussed part of liberalism. There are, of course, many different ways of specifying our basic liberties and guarantees of political equality. Even nonacademics are familiar with debates over individual rights and their limits and the nature of equality, debates that go on within as well as across the boundaries of liberalism. I do not want to take up these familiar debates here, but rather to focus on the second, less familiar dimension of liberalism.

The second part of liberalism—the commitment to public reasonableness—seems likely to be a bit more obscure. It is perhaps more a focus of academic than of popular attention. Nevertheless, practical political debates are sometimes marked by the assertion that a proposed law or policy is nothing but a veiled attempt by some group to impose their religious views on others through political means. The implicit assumption behind such charges is that it is inappropriate to use the law to advance a sectarian agenda. Consider an actual example—the Louisiana law mandating "balanced treatment" in the state's public school classrooms of the theory of evolution and what is referred to as "creation science."[1] My guess is that many ordinary Americans could easily appreciate that the controversy here was not simply over the merits of creation science. Also at stake was the broader question of whether some Louisiana lawmakers were pursuing an agenda that could be justified only by relying on reasons whose force depends on accepting a particular religious perspective.

Among the core features of liberalism as I understand it, is a concern not simply with political outcomes (such as whether important rights are protected at the end of the day), but also with the way that public officials and citizens go about justifying the use of political power. Gerald Gaus has usefully termed this position "justificatory liberalism."[2] At their best, liberals seek political principles that can be publicly justified and widely affirmed by reasonable people in a diverse society. Public justification is important because liberal justice, properly understood, is a social ideal: the liberal ideal of free self-government aspires to a polity in which citizens share a sense of justice, a society in which citizens are critical interpreters and enforcers of liberal values.[3] As Jeremy Waldron puts it, "Liberals demand that the social order should in principle be capable of explaining itself at the tribunal of each person's understanding."[4] Liberal, democratic politics is not only about individual rights and limited government, in other words, it is also about public justification: reason-giving and reason-demanding, and the insistence that power be backed by reasons.

The demand for public reasonableness is especially important where fundamental rights and liberties are at stake, and in the face of a long history of arbitrary and invidious forms of discrimination. The modern Supreme Court has rightly insisted that before the government can infringe on fundamental rights, or before it can subject a "discrete and insular minority" to unequal treatment, a high burden of reasoned justification must be met.[5] The power of the courts helps ensure that the politically weak have a forum in which to contest majority decisions that may rest on mere prejudice, or malice, or lack of concern. In court, the politically weak appear as equals with the representatives of the sovereign state, who must supply reasoned arguments to show that minority interests have not been discounted on arbitrary or invidious grounds.[6] The Constitution, properly understood, calls not only upon the courts, but on executives and legislators as well to assert their own view of the best interpretation of our fundamental law. An aspiration to public reasonableness characterizes what seems to me to be the best version of the theory and practice of liberal constitutionalism: a fundamental political demand is to convert unthinking habits and practices into reasons, or to revise our practices to accord with reasoned standards, and to seek justifications that can be shared by people who disagree reasonably and permanently about their ultimate religious and philosophical ideals.[7]

Liberals do not have a monopoly on the concern with public reasonableness. Some who call themselves "deliberative democrats" also care about the way that people go about justifying the use of political power. The fact is that there is a good deal of overlap and convergence among the views of democratic *liberals* and liberal *democrats*. There is, indeed, much to be learned from the account of public reasonableness offered by deliberative democrats such as Amy Gutmann and Dennis Thompson.[8] These authors usefully emphasize the principles that ought to guide democratic deliberation about the many moral conflicts that are not settled at the level of constitutional design. Gutmann and Thompson sometimes seem to want to offer an alternative to liberalism, but their account seems to me to be a useful extension of liberal public reasonableness rather than an alternative to it.[9]

My aim here is not to engage in product differentiation vis-à-vis "deliberative democrats" or others, but to emphasize the importance of a process of public reasonableness for liberalism. The commitment to public reasonableness helps determine how some substantive political conflicts should be discussed and even settled. In addition, the centrality of public reasonableness for liberalism helps make it clear that liberalism has an important civic dimension: it proposes not simply a set of negative mechanisms for limiting and controlling political power, but also includes positive means for fostering a politics worthy of esteem. This is the case not only because liberal politics protects basic liberties, but also because it fosters a political community united by basic principles and by a commitment to criticizing, debating, and refining those principles in public.

Citizenship and Public Reasonableness

It is worth noting, first of all, that liberal substantive commitments often go hand in hand with the liberal commitment to public reasonableness. This very intimacy may, indeed, obstruct a clear view of the importance of public reasonableness as such. Rawls's masterwork—*A Theory of Justice*—is best known for its defense of substantive principles of liberal justice: the inviolability of certain basic liberties, along with principles of social distribution much more egalitarian than those that characterize American public policy.[10] Perhaps the most controversial and distinctive aspect of Rawls's theory is that part of the distributive principle known as the "difference principle," which says that "the social order is not to establish and secure the more attractive prospects of those better off unless doing so is to the advantage of those less fortunate."[11] What is often (though not always[12]) missed is that Rawls's defense of the egalitarian difference principle is itself tied to his concern that the principles of justice be publicly justifiable to everyone. If we want to discern principles of economic distribution that might be justified to all, the hard part will be to find principles that the least well off in society can accept. Finding principles that can be accepted and affirmed in practice by those who do well according to the chosen scheme will not be difficult. But what can we say to those who wind up at the bottom?[13]

According to the Rawlsian thought experiment, which is supposed to model the demands of fairness, people should think of themselves as choosing principles of justice for a hypothetical society in which they do not know what social position they will occupy, indeed, in which they do not know what sort of family they will be born into or even what sorts of talents or character traits they will have. He suggests that from the point of view of this "original position," people will be led to adopt the difference principle, according to which inequalities are acceptable insofar as they help improve the lot of the least well off in society. Rawls claims that it is not good enough to say to those on the bottom that their poverty is simply the price that must be paid for overall social well-being.

It might seem as though Rawls opts for this distributive principle because he thinks that, from behind a veil of ignorance, people would be averse to risk. Rawls might seem to be saying that in the original position, rational people who are so averse will try to make sure that the worst possible outcome of the "natural lottery" is not all that bad, even if that means lowering the average expected payoff. Some critics have charged that the ascription of risk aversion is an empirical proposition for which Rawls adduces no support.[14] This charge misses the point of Rawls's thought experiment.

Rawls emphasizes the "strains of commitment" that will be felt by someone who finds him or herself at the bottom of a society characterized by principles other than the difference principle: it is asking too much of those who find themselves at the bottom of a system of unequal distribution to accept that their poverty is the price that must be paid for having a well-off society overall. This utilitarian approach requires some "to forego greater life prospects for the sake of others," and in doing so, it seems to treat some individuals as a means to the ends of others.[15] Adopting the difference principle is a way of expressing the commitment of the better off to fair principles that can be justified to all. Anything short of the difference principle will not adequately assure the least well off that their ability to freely assent to the principles of the constitutional order matters as much as anyone else's. The thrust of Rawls's discussion seems to be that nothing short of the difference principle really assures the least well off—who have most reason to suspect that their interests are being discounted—that they are being treated as equals by their fellow citizens. The difference principle most clearly affirms that the good of all matters.[16]

Important aspects of Rawls's approach have been the subject of vigorous disagreement. Rawls himself admits that as things stand, disagreement about what set of economic and social policies would satisfy the "difference principle" is too extensive to be able to regard that principle as a basis for judicial interpretations of existing constitutional guarantees of equality. My aim here is not to defend the whole array of Rawlsian substantive principles, but to use his example to illustrate the close connection between public reasonableness and substantive outcomes. The concern with settling on principles that could be the basis of a reasonable consensus helps shape the selection of basic principles.

The emphasis on public reasonableness and the centrality of public justification to the liberalism I want to defend helps make sense of why and how we can continue to see the idea of a "social contract" as central to liberalism. The idea is not that political legitimacy is based on an actual social contract, in the sense that people are obliged to obey a particular set of laws and institutions because they have actually consented—whether explicitly or tacitly—to be bound by that system of law. As Rawls acutely observes,

> The government's authority cannot . . . be freely accepted in the sense that the bonds of society and culture, of history and social place of origin, begin so early to shape our life and are normally so strong that the right of emigration (suitably qualified) does not suffice to make accepting its authority free, politically speaking, in

the way that liberty of conscience suffices to make accepting ecclesiastical authority free, politically speaking. Nevertheless, we may over the course of life come freely to accept, as the outcome of reflective thought and reasoned judgment, the ideals, principles, and standards that specify our basic rights and liberties, and effectively guide and moderate the political power to which we are subject. This is the outer limit of our freedom.[17]

The point of a contractualist approach to public justification is not to provide opportunities for actual consent which, in any case, would be a rather hollow option for the reasons Rawls indicates ("America—consent to it or leave it!?"). The point, rather, is to suggest that political legitimacy—and our own peace of mind, morally speaking—depend on our ability to discern basic principles of political morality that we believe on reflection could be justified to all, or at least to all reasonable people. The aim is to assure ourselves and our fellow citizens that what we support is a public moral order, a constitution informed by moral principles and a rationale or set of reasons that all reasonable people should be able to accept and affirm publicly before one another. Promoting such a political order is a basic aim of liberalism as I understand it, even if it is an aim whose profile is often lower than the defense of basic liberties. The pursuit of public reasonableness is an end in itself, a way of thinking about the kind of liberal political community we should aim for. This pursuit will itself shape the sorts of institutions and policies that we can accept and affirm in politics.

As citizens of a democratic polity, we are all partly responsible for the way political power gets used. When push comes to shove, political power involves all the coercion and force that modern states can muster. We as citizens help shape the way that power is used, not just the relatively tame power at stake in public school debates or social welfare policy, but the more dramatic forms represented by the FBI, the CIA, and the Bureau of Alcohol, Tobacco, and Firearms. The basic practical question that every citizen faces is what, if anything, ultimately justifies the use of political power? What guiding principles and limits might suffice to make a system of political power morally acceptable, or even worthy of our support? Are there good reasons, not for every discrete act of political power, perhaps, but for the overall order— good reasons for our basic institutions that we can share as a political community? Just how we go about answering these questions is by no means obvious, for serious problems attend the most straightforward approaches.[18]

Preludes to Public Reasonableness

How should we, then, go about justifying the way power is structured and deployed? One straightforward approach is to define an objective human good, such as that offered by Plato in his most famous effort in political theory, *The Republic*. Social justice consists of discerning the character and aptitudes of each individual, and assigning them to social roles based on their innate potential to realize particular aspects of the human good. The just city assigns individuals to their proper roles in a social hierarchy, understood and justified from the point of view of a philosophical understanding of the human good as a whole. Many other philosophical and religious views likewise proceed from the point of view of a comprehensive conception of truth and the human good as a whole.

The problem with this approach, especially in the modern world, is that people disagree about their views of truth as a whole, about man's highest good, about the nature of religious truth, and therefore about the basis of moral and political obligations if these are to be understood as grounded in our highest and broadest conceptions of the human good and truth as a whole. The modern world is characterized by a plurality of religious and philosophical views, a plurality that has often been so deep that many people have believed that people of different faiths and worldviews cannot live together in the same political society.[19]

An alternative approach is provided by John Locke, both in his *Letter Concerning Toleration* and more elaborately in the *Second Treatise*. Without attempting to capture all the nuances of Locke's view, we can nevertheless say that Locke emphasized that people who differ over religion and perhaps other fundamental matters might nevertheless share certain "civil interests" that could furnish an adequate basis for social unity. These civil interests were "things of the body not the soul," and included an interest in an effective rule of law, enforcement agencies to provide security and peace, the protection of basic liberties, and the just possession of property. In the *Second Treatise,* Locke posited certain ideas of natural law and natural rights—inalienable rights to life, liberty and property—that he believed were known to all people of ordinary understanding. To illustrate that an understanding of natural law is innate, Locke speaks of Adam, created as "in full possession" of "strength and reason," and so "capable from the first instant of his being to . . . govern his actions according to the dictates of the law of reason which God had implanted in him."[20] The Lockean social contract takes its bearings from our shared understanding of natural law and natural rights.

The Lockean approach is promising, but the notion that all normal, mature people have access to an easily understood common morality now seems unconvincing. Indeed, it is far from clear that even Locke believed in such a universally understood moral system, for in his more philosophical work Locke famously undercut the notion that there are any innate ideas and he debunked the idea that there are any universal moral judgments.[21] The notion of a shared morality sounds plausible on its face, but in what is this morality grounded, and how do human beings know it? The Lockian solution of discerning certain shared civil interests and a public morality appears promising, but the deficit in his theory is a compelling public account of the philosophical foundations of this shared morality.

The suspicion that there is no shared religious or objective philosophical foundation for a public morality of the sort Locke defended has no doubt fueled charges that Locke's defense of basic rights to "life, liberty, and property" gained its appeal from the fact that it encapsulated the basic interests of the propertied classes of Locke's time. The political morality of the Lockean social contract, according to C.B. Macpherson, is a reflection not of natural law, but of the possessive individualism and class interests of a budding market society. Locke's genius, on this account, was to codify the fundamental principles of competitive individualism and market society. This is the key to his enduring popularity and influence.[22]

Many thinkers embrace the notion that political orders are never really supported by a shared and genuinely justified morality. "Realists" of various stripes argue that common standards of authority rest on interests, and mere collective willfulness, further supported, perhaps, by a dearth of critical reflection. Realism of this sort was forcefully articulated by Locke's social contract predecessor, Thomas Hobbes, who radicalized the fact of our disagreement and extended it much more widely than Locke wished to do. "Whatsoever is the object of any man's appetite or desire," Hobbes insisted, "that is it, which he for his part calleth good." Moral notions such as good and evil, said Hobbes, are "ever used with relation to the person that useth them: there being nothing simply or absolutely so," nor any common meaning "to be taken from the nature of the objects themselves."[23] This sobering teaching suggests that the only way to give moral words a common meaning, and to establish common standards of just and unjust, is for all to defer to some sovereign will that will be authorized to set the terms of political and social cooperation. Political authority has nothing to do with any intrinsic, objective, or extrapolitical standards of reasonableness, for such standards are impossible in Hobbes's realist view. Since there is no possibility of shared moral standards apart from the law made by the sovereign, citizens are not entitled to criticize the law based on moral standards. It is simply absurd, on Hobbes's view, to say that the law is unjust. The law is the only public morality we can have.

The Hobbesian dispensation may be the best we can do. Hobbesian skepticism appears to be a hardheaded realism that is not without its intellectual and political attractions. It certainly represents a way of deflating overblown moralisms that might be used to thwart popular self-government. This skepticism eliminates, however, the possibility of shared limits on sovereign authority (we must obey the sovereign so long as our own lives are not directly threatened). Despite the bracing appeal of the Hobbesian view, many want to believe that we can share a public morality based on certain basic principles of liberty and equality, a public morality that informs the Constitution and helps guide its interpretation. But are these commitments to liberty and equality expressions of nothing more than personal and class preferences and interests? The challenge is to do better than Hobbes while admitting the problems intrinsic to the other alternatives I have mentioned: the problems of diversity and uncertainty that plague the attempts to justify political arrangements based on objective accounts of the highest human good or of religious or philosophical truth.

Public Reason and Political Community

Public reasonableness is an attempt to surmount the hurdles I have mentioned: the disagreement about attempts to capture the entire religious or philosophical truth, the related difficulty of discerning philosophical or religious foundations for a subset of shared political ideas, and the resistance to accepting the Hobbesian invitation to abandon our public moral aspirations in favor of skepticism, will, and power. It seems to me that Rawls has discerned more clearly than anyone else that the public ideals and principles that constitute a practice of public reasoning in and around democratic institutions, when suitably elaborated, are themselves adequate to constitute a public morality, without any further philosophical grounding. A public morality—substantive principles and processes of public justification—can be understood from a public point of view as self-supporting.

Rawls's political liberalism starts with the conviction that reasonable people disagree deeply and permanently about their religious beliefs and philosophical ideals of life. Political liberalism bids us to acknowledge that, given the difficult matters of judgment involved, people may reasonably disagree about the justifiability of even purportedly liberal ideals of life, such as Kantian autonomy or Millian individuality. That the good life is characterized by a pervasive commitment to autonomy is properly regarded as one more sectarian view among others, no more worthy of commanding public authority than other philosophical and religious ideals of life that reasonable people might reject.[24] Political liberalism extends the principle of toleration, as Rawls puts it, from religion to contestable philosophical ideals.[25]

Political liberalism focuses our attention on shared political values without requiring or expecting a thoroughgoing agreement on ultimate ends or a comprehensive set of philosophical values. The basic motive behind political liberalism is the desire to respect reasonable people. Political liberalism asks us not to renounce what we believe to be true, but to acknowledge the difficulty of publicly establishing any single account of truth for the whole of life.[26] When it comes to laying the basis for common political institutions, political liberalism invites us to search for grounds accessible to our reasonable fellow citizens, i.e., appealing to reasons and arguments arising out of common experience and to "generally shared ways of reasoning and plain facts accessible to all." There are upper bounds to how complex arguments can be, and we should avoid the appeal to special metaphysical, philosophical, or religious doctrines. As Rawls puts it in *A Theory of Justice*, which anticipates the principal themes of *Political Liberalism*, the "principles of evidence are adopted for the aims of justice; they are not intended to apply to all questions of meaning and truth. How far they are valid in philosophy and science is a separate matter."[27] To philosophy and science we could add religious inquiry.

The constraint of public justification is an important one. When it comes to justifying the most fundamental political principles, including the most basic individual rights and principled political guarantees, there are good reasons to discount those arguments that are extremely difficult to assess, and that are subject to reasonable disagreement. Basic principles of justice, including those principled grounds for governing access to fundamental political guarantees and opportunities (basic rights and opportunities such as the rights to vote and to marry), should not be based on grounds that could be reasonably rejected by people who hold differing religious and philosophical ideals. We want to believe, after all, that we can share a common citizenship with those who differ from us on many (though of course not all) religious and philosophical matters.

Convictions such as these are far from peculiar to Rawls. Ronald Dworkin has argued that liberals should seek principles that we and our successors "will find easy to understand and publicize and observe; principles otherwise appealing are to be rejected or adjusted because they are too complex or are otherwise impractical in this sense."[28] And while Gutmann and Thompson call themselves "deliberative democrats" and seem to want to distance themselves from Rawls, they reformulate, streamline, and extend (rather than reject) the commitment to public reason. Citizens, say Gutmann and Thompson, "must reason beyond their narrow self-interest" and consider "what can be justified to people who reasonably disagree with them."[29]

My aim here is not to defend Rawls's political liberalism, which, as I have argued elsewhere, is often characterized by an excessive reticence.[30] I want to defend the broader commitment to public reasonableness, which, whether in the hands of Rawls or Gutmann and Thompson, is characterized by a commitment to two basic virtues. First, good citizens should seek to discern and abide by fair terms of cooperation. Reasonable people are, says Rawls, "ready to propose principles and standards as fair terms of cooperation and to abide by them willingly, given the assurance that others will likewise do so."[31] Gutmann and Thompson likewise say that "a deliberative perspective does not address people who reject the aim of finding fair terms for social cooperation; it cannot reach those who refuse to press their public claims in terms accessible to their fellow citizens."[32] Reasonableness and cooperativeness or reciprocity are, obviously, closely bound up here: public reasonableness depends on citizens being willing to deliberate about the fair terms of social cooperation if others will likewise do so. The moral motivation that is counted upon, by Rawls as well as Gutmann and Thompson, lies between altruism on the one side and narrow self-interest on the other; it is a willingness to do your fair share (and to try and discern what is your fair share) in cooperative schemes, including the sovereign political cooperative scheme, so long as others will do the same. At the core of this aspect of public reasonableness, as Gutmann and Thompson stress, lies the virtue of reciprocity.[33]

The second cardinal virtue of public reasonableness is what Rawls calls a willingness to acknowledge the fact of reasonable pluralism, i.e., a willingness to allow that reasonable people who are worthy of respect will nevertheless differ profoundly with respect to their highest conceptions of the human good and their views of religious truth. Rawls's rather stylized way of expressing this is by saying that reasonable people "recognize the burdens of judgment." This is simply the idea that with respect to many longstanding questions of human existence, there is room for reasonable disagreement. By "burdens of judgment," Rawls simply means to indicate that there are commonsense explanations for why reasonable people sometimes disagree: the evidence bearing on a case is often "conflicting and complex, and thus hard to assess and evaluate." Even where we agree that certain considerations are relevant, we may weigh them differently. Concepts and principles are often vague and difficult to apply. The way we assess evidence and weigh moral and political values is to some degree shaped by "our total experience, our whole course of life up until now." Finally, we often have to make intrinsically hard decisions, where we are forced to choose among "cherished values" that cannot all be fully realized.[34] While "burdens of judgment" sounds somewhat exotic, it is hard to dispute Rawls's common sense observations about why reasonable people disagree about many things. We may want to formulate the particulars somewhat differently, as Gutmann and Thompson do, but the important thing is to affirm that public reasonableness has something less than a fully comprehensive scope because of the fact of reasonable disagreement. To acknowledge this, and to affirm its centrality to good citizenship in a liberal polity, is the second basic virtue associated with public reasonableness.

Gutmann and Thompson seem to want to eschew some of Rawls's philosophical apparatus, but what they say is in a similar spirit and, I believe, fully compatible with the foregoing. When we rely on empirical evidence, say Gutmann and Thompson, we should honor "relatively reliable methods of inquiry" and avoid implausible assertions. We should do this so that public discussions can, insofar as possible, be carried on in terms that are mutually acceptable. In addition, it is illegitimate to appeal to "any authority whose conclusions are impervious, in principle as well as practice, to the standards of logical consistency or to reliable methods of inquiry that themselves should be mutually acceptable." That is good, and altogether in the spirit of public reasonableness. The point is not to exclude appeals to religious authority per se, but to exclude appeals to *any* authority impervious to critical assessment from a variety of reasonable points of view. For public power belongs to us all as fellow citizens, and we should exercise it together based on reasons and arguments we can share in spite of our differences. The authority that remains is the authority of reasons we can share in public as reasonable citizens.

Some religious people may reply that their reasons are readily accessible to anyone who leads a good life as defined by their religion, but as Gutmann and Thompson insist, that will not do, for "any claim fails to respect reciprocity if it imposes a requirement on other citizens to adopt one's sectarian way of life as a condition of gaining access to the moral understanding that is essential to judging the validity of one's moral claims." The point of public reasonableness is, after all, to accept the fact of reasonable pluralism, which means trying to discern principles that can be assessed and accepted by individuals who are committed to a wide range of different ways of life.[35] In this way, citizens honor a duty of civility to one another.

Of course, in seeking to understand and negotiate our differences, we shall often need to try to see the world from other peoples' points of view. We certainly cannot assess our duties with respect to the poor, the disabled, the aged, or racial minorities, or anyone whose life and needs appears to be outside the ambit of our personal experiences unless we are prepared to try and put ourselves in their shoes, as best we can. Where, however, people disagree deeply about the way life should be lived, and in fact live very different kinds of lives reflecting these evaluative differences, it will be unreasonable to expect others to adopt our way of life in order for them to gain insight into the truths we believe that life discloses. Would we be willing to return the favor?[36]

In their elaboration of what they call the core value of reciprocity, Gutmann and Thompson seem to me to capture the core demands of public reasonableness, for the reciprocity they seek is a reasoned reciprocity, or as they call it, deliberative reciprocity. Far from challenging the core aspirations of liberal public reason in the name of a more democratic alternative, as some "deliberative democrats" such as Seyla Benhabib claim to do, Gutmann and Thompson extend and elaborate public reason. In particular, they provide a nuanced discussion of how principled conflicts not properly resolvable by the courts should be discussed and negotiated democratically so as to honor our shared commitment to reasoned deliberation. They rightly suggest that we should not become preoccupied with the courts as the sole arenas of public reason.

Once we acknowledge the value of public reasonableness and reciprocity, along with the fact of pluralism, one practical imperative is that we must avoid basing fundamental constitutional principles on grounds that some people in our society could reasonably reject. This is simply to say that no one should expect the Constitution to reflect his or her view of the whole truth, whether that is a religious or a secular truth. Everyone should be satisfied, rather, with a public morality that reflects a core of reasonable agreement on basic principles of political morality, and citizens should try to deliberate about their principled disagreements in ways that honor the nature and limits of the public reasonableness they share.

In this way, liberal public reasonableness seeks to respond to the three preliminary approaches to justification, the three preludes to public reason we refererred to above. A modern Plato or some other thinker who might seek to use political means to advance a comprehensive account of the truth as a whole fails to acknowledge the fact of reasonable disagreement. To Locke we can now say that we do indeed have a public morality based on certain "civil interests" that reasonable people share, and certain principles of liberty and equality that reasonable people are prepared to affirm. These interests and principles, suitably elaborated, along with the norms that grow out of the commitment to public reasonableness itself, can form the core of a public morality on their own, without the need of a further grounding in a particular philosophical or religious tradition. The public morality is freestanding in the sense that it is consistent with, and can be affirmed from, the point of view of a variety of wider and deeper philosophies of life.

The fact is that America does enjoy a widespread consensus on basic guarantees that constitute the core of a political morality. These civil interests and political principles—fair cooperation, civility among citizens who disagree reasonably, a belief in basic liberties, and due process and the rule of law—may not be anyone's idea of the whole truth of the human condition, or the highest good, but people with a variety of different religious and philosophical commitments agree on a core of these ideals. Here, then, is the response to Hobbes: at the foundational level of philosophical argumentation, and when it comes to defining the highest human good, citizens may indeed disagree fairly radically. There is, nevertheless, a reasonable consensus on certain shared matters of urgent concern, which is freestanding in the sense that we do not need to agree in any sort of detail on one comprehensive religious or philosophical outlook. We also disagree about many matters of moral principle, such as abortion, as Gutmann and Thompson rightly emphasize. We are saved from Hobbesianism, however, by an important range of substantive agreement, as well as by the fact that to some degree at least we are prepared to honor certain deliberative procedures and principles where we disagree.

Various questions remain, of course, for this thumbnail sketch does no more than suggest the ambitions of a liberal political order at a high level of abstraction. I have not, for example, specified the nature of "reasonableness" with any level of precision. This, however, is as it should be, for the contours of reasonableness need to be clarified in tackling concrete controversies. Just what it means to be reasonable cannot be specified apart from what seems on reflection to be the limits of a reasonable public confidence with respect to particular practical issues.

Abortion and Slavery

The commitment to "reasonableness" is bound to appear bland, vague, and amorphous. It certainly would be a mistake to think that the contours of reasonableness and unreasonableness could be specified with any clarity in the abstract. The fact is that, to a great extent, many participants in public disputes have been abiding by norms of public reasonableness (more or less) without perhaps doing so self-consciously. So while it may be disappointing to some, trying to think clearly about public reasonableness is not going to allow us to bypass most of the practical deliberation with which we are already familiar, the sort of midlevel deliberation in which Gutmann and Thompson engage.[37] Which is not to say there is nothing distinctive about public reasonableness when compared with the three alternatives mentioned above. Let me say a few words about the demands of public reasonableness, especially with respect to abortion and slavery.

I said above that the affirmation of public reasonableness may push us in a particular direction on substantive issues. If we want to espouse principles that all reasonable people can accept with respect to distributive justice, we should be especially attentive to what will appear reasonable to the least well off in society, and in that way the demands of public reasonableness itself may alter what we think should be the constitutional principles governing property rights and the economy. Or, to take another example, as a matter of personal intellectual conviction I may believe that the whole truth about political economy is found in some combination of the ideas of Milton Friedman, Richard Epstein, and Charles Murray (his work on libertarianism, civil society, and welfare, not race), and I may further believe that were those ideas somehow implemented, we would all—including the poorest among us, at least after a time—be better off. I can also acknowledge, however, that there are ample grounds for reasonable doubts about this, and so it would be unreasonable to seek to impose these ideas by judicial fiat.

But how does public reasonableness play out with respect to abortion? I have suggested elsewhere that with respect to the issue of abortion, the problem is that there are many reasonable arguments on both sides of the debate. The abortion question is so vexing, in a sense, precisely because there are weighty reasons on both sides, and it is easy to see how reasonable people can come down on either side. What does public reasonableness suggest in such a case? On policy issues such as abortion, which seems, as things stand, to come down to a fairly close call between two well-reasoned sets of arguments, the best thing for reasonable people to do might be to acknowledge the difficulty of the argument and the burdens of reason, to respect their opponents and to compromise with them, and to find some middle ground that gives something to each side while the argument goes forward. The right kind of middle ground on abortion would acknowledge both the great weight due to the judgment of the mother and the fact that this choice concerns the continuance of another life. It would, perhaps, honor a woman's choice up to a certain point in the pregnancy and also countenance a variety of measures that would not be permitted were abortion simply a matter of an individual's right to choose. A majority of the Supreme Court settled on this sort of approach in *Planned Parenthood of Southeastern Pennsylvania v. Casey,* where the Court upheld the abortion right while allowing measures to insure that the choice is reflective and informed, at least if these measures do not impose an "undue burden" on a woman's right to choose.[38]

I have suggested that moderation is a virtue justified by the difficulty of occupying a common moral standpoint, or of exercising our common capacity for reasonableness in the same way.[39] When there seem to be good reasons on both sides, and when we have acknowledged the "burdens of reason" or the difficulty that even reasonable people have in making some judgments, the best thing may be to try to give something to both sides, even if on balance one believes one side to be right and the other wrong. It may be that it is not enough to say, as Dworkin does, that the party with the strongest case on balance (no matter how close a call) has a right to win. We sometimes need to go beyond a mere "right to win based on the best case," and acknowledge the reasonableness of the competing case. Public reasonableness—acknowledging as it does the fact of our plurality and the difficulty of exercising our common reason convincingly in public—calls for what Gutmann and Thompson call the virtue of magnanimity: acknowledging the reasonableness of opposing views, and allowing in a self-critical way that not all of the reasoned considerations are on your side.[40] Moderation or magnanimity in the face of very strong competing cases offers a way of honoring not simply the best case but also the case that is very strong. It represents what Gutmann and Thomspon call an "economy of moral disagreement," a way of living with some deep and divisive conflicts that even reasonable people cannot easily resolve.

Now there are those who flatly reject this way of looking at the abortion controversy. John Finnis has denied that the abortion question calls for the sort of moderation and principled compromise I have put forth, arguing that people who attend "strictly to the arguments" without being "distracted by the numbers and respectability of those who propose them" will find that "the issue is not even a close call."[41] Robert George argues likewise, in a critical discussion of Gutmann and Thompson's book, that "the sheer fact that reasonable people disagree about the issue of abortion is no warrant for believing that the pro-life and pro-choice positions are roughly equal in rational strength."[42] This is unarguable, but George seems to me to be rash in endorsing Finnis's conclusions about abortion. I quote at length what George says in support of his claim that abortion is an easy case. Fetal development, he says,

> is concretely *something's (or,* more precisely, *some being's)* natural development from the fetal stage of *its* life into *its* infancy. It is the natural development of a distinct unitary substance—a human being—who begins as a zygote and develops *without substantial change* through the embryonic and fetal stages of its life, then through its infancy, childhood, adolescence, and finally into adulthood. The "similarity" of the "successive stages" in a human being's development consists of nothing less than the fact that these stages are stages in the life *of a particular human being,* with its unity, distinctness, and identity remaining intact through the successive stages of its development. Each of us who is now an adult is the same human being who was at an earlier time an adolescent, a child, an infant, a fetus, an embryo, and a zygote. Thus, however striking one finds the differences between zygote, fetus, and infant, these differences cannot bear the moral weight necessary to warrant the conclusion that killing X at an early enough stage of X's development is not killing a human being, or indeed is not killing X.[43]

The crucial claim here is that what is at stake from the moment of conception and until death is a human being's life. The successive stages of that life do not represent, from a public moral point of view, substantial enough changes to allow us to say that the taking of that life at any stage—or at least in its earliest stages—is anything other than killing a human being.

The problem here is George's contention that the life history that begins as a zygote "develops *without substantial change*" into an adult. I would concede that there is no substantial change *from one moment to the next*, but is it so obvious that there is no *substantial* and indeed *decisive* change when one compares a four-celled zygote and an infant? George is right that there is a continuity in life history from the point of conception until death; it is clear that the embryo is a human being with a particular identity and destiny. Each and every one of us was an embryo once. But it is far from obvious that, with respect to the question of whether a living entity merits the respect of a moral person, there is no substantial difference between a zygote and an infant. The sort of continuity George points to is not enough to establish that an equivalent moral respect is owed to fertilized embryos and more fully developed human beings.

Without rejecting George's position (which indeed I would entertain as possibly true from a metaphysical point of view), it nevertheless seems to me unreasonable to deny that there are also grounds for ascribing substantial moral weight to the development of basic neural or brain functions (the development of sensory capacity, consciousness, or sentience) and viability. Admittedly, because George is right that a human being develops without *substantial* change from one moment to the next, it is difficult to draw lines, difficult to say that here is a person where there was not one before. But the fact that it is difficult to draw sharp temporal lines does not show that there is no substantial moral distinction to be made between the earliest and the latest stages of fetal development.

The decision to have an abortion is a terrible one, to be approached with great seriousness. It seems to me, however, a failure of reasonableness for George and Finnis to assert that abortion is "not even a close call." I would say the same of those who come to the opposite conclusion from George and Finnis, of course, and who say that *that* is not a close call. It is certainly unreasonable for opponents of pro-life arguments to fail to address the strongest versions of those arguments on their own terms. From a public moral point of view, it seems to me we should not write off as frivolous the arguments of either side of this controversy. At the same time, as George rightly suggests, we can (and I hope I do) respect the reasonableness of persons who hold some unreasonable positions, because in many other respects, they exhibit a commitment to reasonableness and goodwill.[44]

What sort of analogy is there, if any, between the issues of abortion and slavery? Abortion is a matter of basic, principled disagreement that calls, I have argued, for a recognition of the reasonableness of both sides of the issue, and for moderation or magnanimity and for principled compromise. Was the same true of debate over slavery in, say, the 1850s? If so, does this impugn public reasonableness, with its suggestion that we must sometimes modify our pursuit of the whole truth as we see it when confronted with reasonable disagreement?

Michael Sandel argues that there is a close analogy between the abortion debate today and the antebellum debate over slavery, and he suggests that this does indeed impugn public reasonableness, and more specifically, Rawls's political liberalism. Abolitionists, he argues, would be debarred by public reason from making the moral case against slavery because

> [r]ooted in evangelical Protestantism, the abolitionist movement argued for the immediate emancipation of the slaves on the grounds that slavery was a heinous sin. Like the argument of some present-day Catholics against abortion rights, the abolitionist case against slavery was explicitly based on a comprehensive moral and religious doctrine.[45]

For similar reasons, Sandel believes that a commitment to public reasonableness means that advocates of gay rights "cannot contest the substantive moral judgment lying behind antisodomy laws, or seek, through open political debate, to persuade their fellow citizens that homosexuality is morally permissible, for any such arguments would violate the canons of liberal public reason."[46]

Sandel's account of public reasonableness seems flawed. He exaggerates, for one thing, the degree to which public reasonableness asks us to "bracket" moral disagreements; indeed, he goes so far as to say that according to this version of liberalism, "government must be neutral on moral and religious questions."[47] This charge is based on faulty premises. Liberal public reasonableness is itself a moral view, and not a political view that purports to be neutral on moral views. Indeed, it is for moral reasons of fairness and civility that public reasonableness asks citizens to honor the authority of reasons they can share in public with others. That does not mean that moral arguments must be excluded from the political arena, only that it is not fair to shape coercive political power based on any reasons whose force depends upon adopting a particular sectarian view, whether that sectarian view is a religious doctrine or a philosophical vision. Citizens committed to public reasonableness would be concerned to try to discern and debate a public morality that could be shared by all reasonable people, and they would recognize that in doing so they were helping to bring about a good political community. Public reasonableness stands for a moral agenda through and through. It does not avoid moral controversies as such; rather, it settles some of them and prescribes ways of dealing with and negotiating those that are not easily settled but that should be the subject of ongoing debate and deliberation.

Another way in which Sandel's criticisms rest on misunderstanding is with respect to the charge that public reason restricts speech. Here, Sandel has distinguished company. Seyla Benhabib charges that liberal public reason is conceived "not as a process of reasoning among citizens but as a regulative principle imposing limits upon how individuals, institutions, and agencies ought to reason about public matters."[48] Stephen Carter likewise argues that the liberal emphasis on public reason effectively silences seriously religious people in politics, because they are debarred from offering religious arguments.[49]

Advocates of public reasonableness do not advocate restrictions on political speech, as these critics might seem to imply. No one is suggesting that the contours of liberal public reason should be used to define the limits of constitutional rights to free speech. Public reason helps define a moral ideal, not a legal requirement. The point of stressing the political authority of public reasonableness is to point out that when it comes to shaping basic principles of justice, which will limit and direct the fearsome coercive powers of the modern state, it is fair and appropriate to try to discern reasons and evidence whose force can be appreciated by our reasonable fellow citizens whose larger religious and philosophical views may not wholly correspond to our own. If people disagree with the aspiration to be governed by public reason, then of course, they should say so and we should talk about it. Speech is not the issue. The issue is, on what grounds may we justify coercive political powers? If some people nevertheless feel "silenced" or "marginalized" by the fact that some of us believe that it is wrong to seek to shape basic liberties on the basis of religious or metaphysical claims, I can only say "grow up!"

Do Sandel and Benhabib regard religious reasons and arguments as acceptable grounds for fashioning constitutional essentials? That is, leaving aside the red herring of permissible *speech,* would Benhabib or Sandel consider it permissible for a state to pass a law restricting a minority's religious worship on the basis of straightforwardly religious arguments? Liberals say that this is wrong. It is wrong not only as an infringement on religious liberty, but also wrong as a violation of the duty of civility according to which citizens owe each other reasons that they can share when determining such basic political matters.

Benhabib's own Enlightenment-inspired project would seem to lead in the same direction as the liberalism of public reason. Against Iris Marion Young, Michel Foucault, and others, Benhabib seems to defend a commitment to political justification based on public reasons that we can hold in common. Straightforward reliance on naked self-interest, or prejudice, or passionate hatred, or religious faith will surely, in Benhabib's scheme, be regarded as inappropriate ways of justifying the use of power. Is this not as exclusionary and constraining as Rawls? Does not Benhabib "silence" not only the religious fanatic but also the nakedly self-interested individual every bit as much as Rawls? Stephen Carter, for example, wants to welcome religious discourse in the public square because it is a source of passion instead of mere reason. Would Benhabib agree with this? My guess is that Benhabib's disagreement with liberal public reasonableness—leaving aside the peculiarities of Rawls's view—is far less severe than she seems to believe.

Sandel seems genuinely worried that our political discourse does not adequately engage religious disagreements. Does Sandel believe that by talking about religion in the public square we can settle the question of religious truth to the satisfaction of our reasonable fellow citizens? If we delay the project of political justification until we work through the question of religious truth, we shall never get to politics at all. Or is Sandel just supposing that the sort of moral arguments with respect to nuclear deterrence offered by the Catholic bishops, or natural law arguments on homosexuality, are in some basic way at odds with public reasonableness? Interestingly enough, the bishops and the Catholic scholars and citizens who discuss public moral issues in America today insist that their arguments are grounded in philosophical reasons that can be assessed and appreciated by all. I am not sure they all fully accept the political authority of public reasonableness, but they at least insist that all they espouse in politics can be fully justified without resort to theology, or any specifically religious premises, or any claims of authority impervious to common reason.

Note finally that in some circumstances, religious *speech* is perfectly justifiable in politics. The point of public justification is that when it comes to *deciding* upon the fair grounds of coercion, we are obliged by respect for the freedom and equality of our fellow citizens to offer them grounds that they should be able to accept: political power is the shared property of the political community. Liberal citizens should acknowledge the political authority of reasons and arguments that can be shared by their reasonable fellow citizens; this does not mean that they must never speak in public about politics in religious terms. It means that at the culmination of public discussion—at least when basic matters of justice are at stake—good citizens will invoke, and attest to the authority of, grounds that can be shared by a diverse community in public.[50] Good liberal citizens, I want to affirm, aspire to a political community in which they can justify the constitutional basics to one another in terms they can share. Liberalism properly understood is not just about the protection of individual liberty; it is about the aspiration to public reasonableness.

Sometimes Benhabib and Sandel write as though politics is all talk, but it is about more than talk. Political decisions will almost always have to be made *before* the conversation is over, before a consensus is reached about many matters. We must decide what to do even though people will not agree about many things, most particularly about their ultimate religious and philosophical ideals. Political decisions will, moreover, be backed by all the terrible coercive power of the state. It is for these reasons that liberal contractualists think it important to delimit the appropriate grounds of justification. Reasonable disagreement about some things seems to be a fact of the human condition, but we need to get on with the business of politics, and hopefully we can get on with it as a political community characterized by civility and mutual respect. Liberals do not wish to close down wide-ranging political discussion, but only to insist that citizens owe each other justifications that they can share in public.

A final point about the relationship between the liberal delimitation of public reason and democratic deliberation. To the extent that public reasonableness encourages citizens and public officials to focus on arguments and reasons that can be shared by reason-

able people in public, it is likely that the result is not less deliberation (as Sandel and Benhabib seem to say) but more. If reasonably
contestable religious principles and ultimate philosophical ideals
are held to be illegitimate grounds on which to settle constitutional
basics, then there will be less political speech about *these* matters
than otherwise in politics. This does not mean, however, that there
will be less democratic deliberation. It may be that real, constructive deliberation about some matters will be possible only because
other matters are not part of (or at least not at the center of) the
political agenda. In a diverse polity such as ours, we are able to
have a sustained and reasonably constructive debate about health
care reform or crime only because we have agreed to disagree
about other matters, such as religious truth, which are arguably
more important. The constructiveness of much political deliberation may depend, therefore, on removing some matters from the
agenda.[51]

None of this means that religious speech is suppressed, and
when the question of abortion arises in the health care debate,
religion may come closer to the political surface. Even there,
however, people generally recognize the inappropriateness of sectarian religious appeals, and the discussion is generally focused on
matters of shared concern and public assessment: Is the fetus a
moral person? Is viability really a crucial turning point in fetal
development? Is the right to abortion contributing to a culture in
which human life is devalued? Pro-lifers such as George and Finnis
in principle accept the political authority of public reason, and in
this they are typical, rather than academic eccentrics. Contrary to
the assertions of Sandel and Carter, it is far from obvious that the
vast majority of religious people disagree with the basic commitment to public reasonableness in politics.[52]

But what about slavery? Sandel says that with respect to slavery,
the liberalism of public reason is pushed into the position of
Stephen Douglas, who felt that because slavery was a matter of
such intense disagreement at the time of the founding, it had to be
regarded from the point of view of basic constitutional principles

as simply off the national agenda, left to citizens to deal with in their individual states. Sandel insists that since the abolitionist opposition to slavery, like the opposition to abortion and the defense of gay rights, is "explicitly based on a comprehensive moral and religious doctrine," the liberalism of public reason would silence these moral voices, thereby creating "a moral void that opens the way for the intolerant and the trivial and other misguided moralisms."[53]

Once again, Sandel does not seem to me to have these matters quite right. It really makes no difference to public reasonableness whether particular arguments against slavery are, at some level, "rooted" in religious arguments. At some level, virtually *every* moral argument could be said to grow out of, or originate in, a religious development or a dispute among theologians. Moral arguments have different aspects and can be looked at in different lights. Many moral arguments also have long pedigrees, and no doubt many or most could be traced back to antecedents that were embedded in theology. It was not that long ago that, for most people, religious and moral arguments were hardly distinguishable. The very principle of religious toleration, for example, is often said to have Protestant origins. Locke defended religious toleration on a variety of grounds, some religious, some secular. The first line of his *Letter Concerning Toleration* argues that toleration is "the Chief characteristical mark of the true church."[54] Some scholars examine Locke's political teaching and his interpretation of scripture and argue that he is a Socinian, and that his argument for toleration is in some sense rooted in his Socinianism.[55]

Does this mean that Locke's commitment to toleration was rooted in his religious views? Of course. Does that mean it must be removed from the liberal corpus? Of course not. The force of many of Locke's arguments does not depend on his holding a particular religious view (the argument that princes have no special expertise in matters of religion, that persecution would cause violence and mere outward conformity with orthodox views, and so forth). At the same time some religious people, on account of their religious convictions, will reject Locke's arguments. If various religions regard toleration as heretical, then before liberalism and public reasonableness can begin to take hold, those religions will have to accommodate themselves to toleration in their own way. That does not mean that toleration is rooted in a *particular* religion, only that it is not compatible with all religions. There is nothing surprising about that or any way to get around it (or any reason we should try). The whole point of trying to demarcate a sphere of *public* reasonableness is that citizens have larger comprehensive views that they can disagree about, and that they need not settle before getting on with public moral argument.

The situation with respect to antislavery arguments is no different. At some level, many people's beliefs about why slavery is wrong will "grow out of" or be "rooted in" religious considerations. But the force of antislavery arguments does not depend upon adopting a particular religious point of view (though, here again, some religious points of view will, perhaps, contribute to the acceptance of slavery).

Sandel asserts that the liberal commitment to public reasonableness leads to Stephen Douglas's position on slavery. Douglas held that the framers of the Constitution disagreed profoundly about slavery, and therefore did not settle it as a matter of basic constitutional principle, and indeed excluded it from the national agenda, leaving it to the states to deal with as a local matter. But would a proponent of public reasonableness have been driven to Douglas's view?

It certainly is the case that Douglas's arguments (which were about constitutional interpretation, first and foremost, but informed by certain principles of political morality) were, in the main at least, public arguments, but that does not mean he had a monopoly on public arguments. Sandel ignores or misses the fact that Abraham Lincoln's profound opposition to slavery was also rooted in public considerations. He allowed that some people had doubts that blacks and whites were equal in all respects, but he insisted that with respect to fundamental equality—the Lockean rights of self-ownership, which included being one's own master and enjoying the fruits of one's own labor—there could be no doubt about the equality of the races.[56] To say that blacks and whites are equally independent moral beings, with an equal right to be free, to lead one's own life, and an equal capacity to direct one's own life and follow the rules of justice, is indeed a moral position, but contrary to Sandel, it is not a moral position that is in any way barred by political liberalism. Lincoln may have invoked God in some of his most important public statements, but he fully justified his moral opposition to slavery in public moral terms. He went so far, of course, as to say that if slavery was not wrong, nothing was wrong.

But will not liberal public reasonableness look down upon those who in addition to public reasons also invoke further religious grounds and considerations? Not necessarily. Not given the enormous injustice of slavery and the need to rally opposition to it. Not if doing so is efficacious in bolstering public arguments with additional considerations designed to show that slavery is not only unjust (in public terms) but also un-Christian. Not unless extrapolitical arguments are being advanced so as to suggest a wider specifically sectarian agenda, as for example if one were to say, "first we are going to get rid of slavery, and then we are going to impose a Christian republic." Even then, given the enormity of slavery, a sensible political liberal might (depending on the array of political forces) embrace an alliance against slavery with religious fanatics while expressing opposition to their wider agenda.

Of course there were abolitionists who saw the opposition to slavery as part of a larger Christian agenda for America. Most people in America in the mid-nineteenth century did not altogether distinguish their political morality from their religious views. This was a time when most Americans believed that republicanism was in some way "rooted in" Protestantism. Times have changed. It is now easier for people to distinguish between religious and public moral arguments. It is difficult for me to see why Sandel seems to want to revive those close linkages, or why he thinks doing so would improve the quality of public deliberation or political community in late twentieth-century America.

Public reasonableness is part of a liberal political ideal: we should hope for and aim at a society in which we can be governed by reasons we can share. Public reason does not specify a set of absolute constraints on speech under all circumstances. Sometimes, under nonideal circumstances, invoking nonpublic reasons on behalf of a cause that is itself publicly justifiable is the right thing to do.

But, finally, would liberal public reason have to regard slavery as a "hard case," like abortion, and therefore meriting the same sort of principled compromise that I have defended with respect to abortion? There is every reason to be leery of any general rules with respect to the question of how we should treat such singular issues as abortion and slavery. There is something a little slick in drawing quick analogies between slavery and abortion in order to impugn public reason. Without having investigated the historical context with any thoroughness, I must speak tentatively. Projecting myself back to say, 1857, it seems quite doubtful to me that the merits of the arguments for slavery would have appeared in as reasonable a light as do both sides in today's abortion debate (or as does the weaker side in today's abortion debate, whichever side one takes that to be). Of course, it is difficult (for this Massachusetts Yankee) to adopt the perspective of a reasonable pro-slavery Southerner of good will. I suppose there were some whose defense of slavery, coupled perhaps with opposition to "wage slavery" in the North, amounted to a reasoned public case, worthy of some sort of respect. That does not mean that the sort of principled compromise that I have suggested with respect to abortion would be justified in regard to slavery. For as Robert George points out, respect may sometimes be owed to persons who in general exhibit reasonableness and good will, but not to some position they have adopted, which one regards as so deeply misguided and wrong as to be unworthy of respect.

This is where the difference between the slavery and abortion cases seems to lie. In my view, reasonable people come to different views on abortion, partly on account of the fact that there really is a reasoned case to be made on each side. Contrary to George and Finnis, it does not seem to me that the abortion case is, in fact, "not even a close call;" abortion does not seem to me an easy case for those who look at the merits undistracted by extraneous considerations. Indeed, I think that the people whose understanding is clouded are those on either side who think that, based on public reasons and evidence, it is an easy case.

With respect to the purportedly "reasonable person of good will" who is pro-slavery, on the other hand, I would be disposed to adduce the sorts of considerations that George adduces with respect to the pro-choice position on abortion. He proposes that "cultural circumstances or other factors make it possible for reasonable people of goodwill" to be "mistaken about even serious moral evils when ignorance, prejudice, self-interest, and other factors that impair sound moral judgment are prevalent in a culture or subculture."[57] Because of how I see the merits of the abortion case, I do not need to suppose that the understanding of reasonable people on either side is impaired, unless they refuse to allow that on abortion there are good arguments on both sides. George's suggestions seem very apposite, on the other hand, with respect to any reasonable people of good will who supported human slavery as it was known in the American South. If decent people of good will supported human slavery on due reflection, then one can only suppose that they were victims of circumstances and traditions that were indeed morally perverse. Contrary to Sandel's suggestion, these considerations suggest only that one would want to treat such *persons* with due respect, insofar as one could, not that one would compromise with or act magnanimously toward the evil practice they erroneously support.

It is worth emphasizing that just because people come to agree on the political authority of public reason does not mean they are going to have an easier time settling particular disagreements. Public reason can often be invoked on opposite sides of vexing issues. The basic point is that public reason provides the appropriate terms of argument when basic issues of justice are at stake, not that the resort to public reason necessarily settles anything. Just because we all agree on the authority of public reason, that does not mean we are going to agree on where it leads, or how public reason should be weighed.

There are obviously some vexing issues here, for it is not easy to know to what extent one's moral disagreements with others, especially with others who exhibit good will and a desire to honor public reason, is colored by one's particular experiences, and the way one lives one's life. All we can do is be as reflective and self-critical as we can, listen to opposing arguments, and try to give as much credence as seems reasonable to those with whom we disagree. If our reflective conscientious moral attitudes are partly the product of our personal histories and the way we lead our lives, this is indeed, as George suggests, a sobering consideration. It is not, however, a consideration that impugns the value of public reasonableness; to the contrary, it would seem to strengthen the case for the core characteristic of public reasonableness, which is the conviction that we should be sensitive to the difference between what seems *true* to me and my group, and *what can publicly be seen to be reasonable by the many reasonable people and groups that constitute society*. Critics such as Sandel want to seem to cast aside this sort of distinction, and the particular sensitivities that go with it. He seems to want to urge people to march into the political arena armed with their conceptions of the truth as a whole, pressing those conceptions with vigor and without inhibition. This seems to me a recipe for atavism, a way of ignoring or failing adequately to acknowledge central features of the modern world that have been learned the hard way, and over the course of centuries: we can and should accept the fact of reasonable disagreement while seeking a community of public principles.

Conclusion

There are a plethora of other issues that might usefully be considered from the perspective of public reasonableness. I have argued elsewhere, for example, that natural law arguments against homosexuality either fail straightforwardly, or, if these arguments can in reason be maintained, that will only be on grounds that are so subject to reasonable disagreement as to be inappropriate for denying fundamentally equal rights and opportunities to homosexuals.[58] Space does not permit me to elaborate further.

It seems to me, in conclusion, that in spite of the criticisms to which it has been subject, the ideal of public reasonableness should retain a central place in our political morality. It is not a way of bypassing or easily resolving moral conflicts. It may, indeed, make some moral questions harder to deal with, for it may require us to extend forms of respect to persons and positions we believe to be in error. It holds out the possibility, however, that people for whom disagreement about our highest ideals and the truth as a whole is a permanent condition, might nevertheless share a political community based on a reasonableness they can share. This seems the best we can do, and, as a way of conceptualizing our shared political project and of proceeding with it, it seems to me superior not only to the political views that preceded it, but also to those offered by its critics.

Notes

1. See the opinions of Justices Brennan, Powell, and Scalia in *Edwards v. Aguillard*, 482 U.S. 578 (1987).
2. Gerald F. Gaus, *Justificatory Liberalism: An Essay on Epistemology and Political Theory*. New York: Oxford University Press, 1996.
3. I have tried to develop a version of this ideal at some length in *Liberal Virtues: Citizenship, Virtue, and Community in Liberal Constitutionalism*. Oxford, UK: Clarendon Press, 1992.
4. Jeremy Waldron, "Theoretical Foundations of Liberalism," *Philosophical Quarterly* 37 (1987), 127–50.
5. *U.S. v. Carolene Products*, 304 U.S. 144 (1938).
6. For a good example of the right sort of approach, see the opinion for the Court, and Justice Stevens's concurring opinion in *Cleburne v. Cleburne Living Center*, 473 U.S. 432 (1985).

7. I have tried to defend such a version of liberal constitutionalism in *Liberal Virtues*. Representatives of liberal contractualism include John Rawls (see works cited below), T. M. Scanlon (see esp. "Contractualism and Utilitarianism," in *Utilitarianism and Beyond*, ed. A. Sen and B. Williams [Cambridge, UK: Cambridge University Press, 1982]), Thomas Nagel (see "Moral Conflict and Political Legitimacy," *Philosophy and Public Affairs*, 16 [summer 1987]: 215–40), and Bruce A. Ackerman (see *Social Justice in the Liberal State* [New Haven, Conn: Yale University Press, 1980]) and "Why Dialogue?" *Journal of Philosophy*, 86, no. 1 [1989], 5–22). There are, of course, important differences among these writers.

8. Amy Gutmann and Dennis Thompson, *Democracy and Disagreement*. Cambridge, Mass.: The Belknap Press of Harvard University Press, 1996.

9. See their discussion of reciprocity in *Democracy and Disagreement*, ch. 2. It is also worth noting that Gutmann and Thompson join Rawls in immunizing basic liberties from democratic deliberation, and not only those basic liberties that help constitute a fair democratic process. See ch. 6, esp. pp. 210–11.

10. John Rawls, *A Theory of Justice*. Cambridge, Mass.: The Belknap Press of Harvard University Press, 1971.

11. Ibid., p. 75.

12. See the acute discussion by Scanlon, "Contractualism and Utilitarianism."

13. This requires that we concede, as we should, that even the choice of free market economic principles is a collective choice to distribute economic goods according to certain mechanisms and principles. Some classical liberals miss this point. See, for example, Friederich Hayek, *Law, Legislation, and Liberty, vol. 2: The Mirage of Social Justice*. University of Chicago Press, 1978, and Judith Shklar's rejoinder in *Faces of Injustice*, New Haven, Conn.: Yale University Press, 1990.

14. See Brian Barry, *The Liberal Theory of Justice*. Oxford, UK: Oxford University Press, 1973, ch. 9.

15. Rawls, *A Theory of Justice*, p. 180, and see section 29 generally.

16. Ibid., esp. pp. 176–78.

17. John Rawls, *Political Liberalism*. New York: Columbia University Press, 1993, p. 222.

18. All of this, obviously, owes much to Rawls.

19. See Rawls, *Political Liberalism*, pp. xxi–xxiv.
20. John Locke, *Second Treatise* ed. Peter Laslett. New York: Mentor, 1963, par 56, p. 347.
21. See Locke's *An Essay Concerning Human Understanding*, ed. Peter H. Nidditch, Oxford: Oxford University Press, 1975, Book I and ch. 28.
22. C. B. Macpherson, *The Political Theory of Possessive Individualism: Hobbes to Locke*. New York: Oxford University Press, 1979, esp. pp. 270–72.
23. Thomas Hobbes, *Leviathan*, ed. C. B. Macpherson. Harmondsworth, UK: Penguin, 1968, Part I, ch. 6, p. 120.
24. Rawls, *Political Liberalism*, pp. 77–81.
25. Ibid., p. 154.
26. See the discussion of the "burdens of judgment," ibid., pp. 54–58.
27. Rawls, *A Theory of Justice*, pp. 132 and 214.
28. Ronald Dworkin, *Taking Rights Seriously*. Cambridge, Mass.: Harvard University Press, 1977, p. 166.
29. Gutmann and Thompson, *Democracy and Disagreement*, pp. 2 and 255.
30. Stephen Macedo, "The Politics of Justification," *Political Theory*, vol. 18 (May, 1990), pp. 280–304, and "Transformative Constitutionalism and the Case of Religion: Defending the Moderate Hegemony of Liberalism," *Political Theory*, 26 (February 1998), pp. 56–89.
31. Rawls, *Political Liberalism*, p. 49.
32. Gutmann and Thompson, *Democracy and Disagreement*, p. 55.
33. I have argued elsewhere that this motivation is nurtured by the right sorts of "civil society institutions": institutions intermediate between the individual and the state nurture the sorts of "in-between" motivations of cooperativeness and reciprocity on which a healthy liberal democratic social order depends. See my discussion in "Community, Diversity, and Civic Education: Toward a Liberal Political Science of Group Life," *Social Philosophy and Policy*, 13 (winter 1996), pp. 240–68.
34. Rawls, *Political Liberalism*, pp. 56–57.
35. Gutmann and Thompson, *Democracy and Disagreement*, p. 567.
36. There are obviously some tough questions here. For further discussion of these points, see my "Liberal Civic Education and Religious

Fundamentalism: The Case of God vs. John Rawls?" *Ethics*, 105 (April 1995), pp. 468–96, and "Transformative Constitutionalism and the Case of Religion."

37. The notion of "reasonableness" is philosophically fuzzy but in practice indispensable. It might be interesting to think about the many ways that "reasonableness" gets invoked in a variety of practical contexts. There is the "reasonable man" standard in law, of course, and in the affairs of common life, as well as in politics, we constantly rely on the sense that there are roughly shared standards of what constitute reasonable precautions, reasonable risks, reasonable care, and so forth. After an American military base in Saudi Arabia was bombed, Secretary of Defense William Cohen concluded that the general in charge of the base had not, under the circumstances, taken reasonable precautions against terrorist attacks. Such judgments are complex and partly contextual, but everyone has the sense that we can make them. Reasonableness almost always implies a range of reasonable discretion, but it also implies the possibility of discerning unreasonable ranges of excess or of negligence. My sense is that when some critics complain about Rawls's promiscuous use of "reasonableness" they are making the mistake of expecting philosophical precision when all that is possible is a certain confidence arising from the practical indispensability of the notion.

38. *Planned Parenthood of Southeastern Pennsylvania v. Casey*, 505 U.S. 833 (1992).

39. For an account that pushes these difficulties much further and, as a consequence, argues for the importance of a model of "mediation," see Fred M. Frohock, "The Boundaries of Public Reason," *American Political Science Review*, 91, no. 4 (December 1997), pp. 833–44.

40. See Gutmann and Thompson, *Democracy and Disagreement,* pp. 79–80.

41. John Finnis, "Is Natural Law Theory Compatible with Limited Government?" in *Natural Law, Liberalism, and Morality*, ed. Robert P. George. Oxford, UK: Clarendon Press, 1996, p. 18.

42. Robert P. George, "Law, Democracy, and Moral Disagreement," *Harvard Law Review*, 110 (1997), 1396.

43. Ibid., pp. 1396–97.

44. Ibid., p. 1398.

45. Michael Sandel, "Political Liberalism" (Review of Rawls's Political Liberalism), *Harvard Law Review*, 107 (1994), p. 1791.

46. Ibid.

47. Ibid, p. 1793.

48. Seyla Benhabib, "Deliberative Rationality and Models of Democratic Legitimacy," *Constellations: An International Journal of Critical and Democratic Theory*, 1 (April 1994), p. 36.

49. Stephen Carter, *Culture of Disbelief: How American Law and Politics Trivialize Religious Devotion*. New York: Basic Books, 1993.

50. So far as Rawls is concerned, this is all made a bit clearer in "The Idea of Public Reason Revisited," *University of Chicago Law Review*, 64, no. 3 (1997).

51. See Stephen Holmes's provocative "Gag Rules or the Politics of Omission," in *Constitutionalism and Democracy*, ed. J. Elster and R. Slagstad. Cambridge, UK: Cambridge University Press, 1988, pp. 19–58.

52. See the important study by Alan Wolfe, *One Nation, After All*. New York: Viking, 1998.

53. Sandel, "Political Liberalism," p. 1794.

54. John Locke, *A Letter Concerning Toleration*, ed. J. H. Tully. Indianapolis, Ind.: Hackett, 1985; originally published 1689.

55. See Tully's introduction to Locke's *Letter*, ibid.

56. *The Lincoln-Douglas Debates of 1858*, ed. Robert W. Johannsen. New York: Oxford University Press, 1965.

57. George, "Law, Democracy, and Moral Disagreement," p. 1400.

58. Stephen Macedo, "Homosexuality and the Conservative Mind," and "Reply to Critics" (Robert P. George, Gerard V. Bradley, and Hadley Arkes), *Georgetown Law Journal*, 84 (December 1995), pp. 261–300 and 329–38.

Robert P. George and Christopher Wolfe

Natural Law and Public Reason

Rawls and Macedo and Public Reason

Stephen Macedo, in his *Liberal Virtues*[1] and in a number of separately published articles, has defended a liberal doctrine of public reason, one which he considers to be in line with John Rawls's conception.[2] According to Macedo, liberalism asks us to consider principles of justice from an impartial point of view, one capable of discerning reasons that should be acceptable to everyone concerned, at least insofar as they are being reasonable. This requires reasoned arguments that are (1) publicly stated, (2) openly debated, and (3) widely accepted.[3] The requirement of public justification demands that we filter out reasons and arguments whose grounds are (1) private, (2) too complex to be widely understood, and (3) otherwise incapable of being widely appreciated by reasonable people.[4]

The conditions or grounds of public justification are three. First, there is the fact of reasonable pluralism: people typically and "reasonably" disagree on important issues, largely as a result of what Rawls has labeled the "burdens of judgment." Second, public justification is required by our respect for people as free and equal moral beings (if they pass certain threshold tests of reasonableness). And third, public justification makes it possible to distinguish intractable moral and philosophical issues from problems that are more urgent (from a liberal perspective) and easier to grapple with; for example, securing basic liberties and establishing fair principles of distribution.[5]

There is much that is attractive in Macedo's thought about public reason. For example, a political theory that elevates reasoned deliberation above mere struggles over interests, power, and unreasoned desires is commendable. Moreover, Macedo's conception of public reason is superior to other liberal conceptions, including that of Rawls, inasmuch as it accepts the public accessibility of arguments that reflect a genuine concern for human character or virtue (albeit in what we consider to be a somewhat truncated form).

Problems with Liberal Public Reason

We have seen that public reason, in Macedo's understanding, requires that arguments providing public justification not be (1) private, (2) too complex to be widely understood, and (3) otherwise incapable of being widely appreciated by reasonable people. Accepting for the moment the requirement that arguments be "public," let us ask what it means to say that an argument may not be either "too complex" or "otherwise incapable of being widely appreciated by reasonable people," which together presumably make up (at least part of) the requirement that arguments be "publicly accessible."

When is an otherwise perfectly reasonable argument "too complex"? When is an argument "incapable of being widely appreciated by reasonable people"? When is such an argument not "publicly accessible"? Macedo is apparently relying on what he takes to be commonsense notions of what these mean, without explaining them in any detail; but that won't do. There are no agreed upon or commonsense meanings of these phrases. Rather, people's disagreements about what is or is not "too complex" or "publicly accessible" will almost certainly replicate their substantive moral disagreement regarding the underlying matters in dispute.

To pass muster under the liberal doctrine of public reason, does an argument have to be "simple" enough (presumably the opposite of "complex") so that all (or virtually all) citizens understand it, or that most of them do so (and does that mean a large, rather than a bare, majority), or that the "educated" element of the citizenry does so? If *all* the citizens have to understand it, then the doctrine is in trouble, because it is difficult to imagine many serious arguments on difficult issues of basic justice that all (or even virtually all) citizens would understand. Some people lack the requisite intelligence to follow complex chains of moral reasoning; many more have not been educated well enough to be able to do so. And it is easy to imagine important political arguments that *most* citizens would have great difficulty understanding. But it would be foolish, and sometimes literally impossible, to remove from politics issues that necessarily and unavoidably generate such arguments.

Are we to construct some idealized figure—something like the law's "reasonable man"—i.e., a person of "average" intelligence with an "average" education (whatever that would mean)? What are the standards according to which such an idealized figure should be constructed? Or is it that the arguments should be intelligible to well-educated people, who would then serve as representatives of all those who share their views, though perhaps to widely ranging degrees of sophistication? If so, how should we define "well-educated"? And then we might ask whether the well-educated people of a given society or era might not accept as rational some pretty irrational positions. (People typically find the possibility of gross moral error by a putatively enlightened cultural elite easy to accept when they look at the well-educated people of past or foreign societies, but people are perhaps less ready to admit the possibility of error in the case of their own societies, especially when they themselves are part of the elite and share its dominant views.) And, if we go down the road of relying on educated people, haven't we, at that point, established a strongly elitist—and not very *public*—doctrine of "public reason"?

Moreover, would it be unreasonable to indulge a suspicion that, if liberal public reason is adopted as a standard, those who are most adept at manipulating language and symbols—members of what Irving Kristol labels the "knowledge class"—are going to end up with a disproportionate share of the power to define what can and cannot be admitted into public discourse and decision-making on the most fundamental issues facing a society?

Whether an argument is "publicly accessible" certainly cannot be determined simply on the basis of whether people happen to agree with it (rendering it accessible) or disagree with it (leading to the conclusion that it is inaccessible). That would make any conventional view ipso facto publicly accessible, irrespective of how irrational it truly was, and any unpopular or unconventional view ipso facto not publicly accessible, irrespective of how rational it truly was, which would make reform and improvement of public views excessively difficult.

Does public accessibility have to do only with the logical quality of the argument itself? Should we consider the rhetorical effectiveness of arguments put forward on behalf of a position? Might it not be the case that most people in a given society agree with a particular argument—creating the impression that it is publicly accessible—on irrational grounds? Do we factor in (either positively or negatively) the "customary ways of thinking" in a society? Does the existence of a custom provide an argument that the judgment embodied in the custom is publicly accessible, or does its being "merely a matter of custom" undermine its claim to being a genuinely rational judgment?

And, finally, does the argument that public arguments must be "publicly accessible" itself have to meet the standard of public accessibility? After all, Rawls's own argument in defense of the liberal public reason doctrine in *Political Liberalism* is highly complex and controversial. It can hardly be considered more accessible than some of the arguments that the doctrine is meant to exclude as grounds of legislative action (e.g., the argument that claims to abortion rights are trumped by the right to life of unborn human beings).

At the start, then, there are a whole series of ambiguities about what is to count as the standard of public reason. Let us turn now to another set of questions, by looking at Macedo's critique of natural law from the viewpoint of liberal public reason.

Macedo's Critique of Natural Law Theory

Macedo's primary, but not his only, claim against natural law ideas is that they fail to meet the requirements of public justification. This is due, he says, to the "large gap between the first principles of natural law and actual moral norms."[6] To get from one to the other requires much work by a process of moral inference, which requires a wisdom or reasonableness not found in everyone or even in most people. Therefore, relying on such arguments is contrary to the equality of respect embodied in liberal canons of public justification. Or, he suggests, natural law thinking can save itself from elitism by appealing to mere popular prejudices about how human beings should behave, thus transforming itself into an "unreasoned populism."[7]

Natural law theorists would respond that there is sometimes, but not always, a "large gap" between the first principles of natural law and actual moral norms. In the natural law theory of Thomas Aquinas, for example, there is a movement of some sort from first principles of natural law (e.g.,"such and so is a good to be done and pursued. . .") to actual moral judgments that guide choice and action in concrete cases ("this item should be returned to the person from whom I borrowed it"). The first, most general precepts are known by (or can easily come to be known by) everyone, at least as abstract principles. Even some moral norms (e.g, those at a high degree of generality) are normally known to all, but our knowledge of them and willingness to abide by them can be corrupted by contrary passions, vicious customs, bad habits, and so forth.[8] (Aquinas himself gives the example of theft not being considered wrong among the Germanic tribes, on Caesar's account of their beliefs and customs.[9]) As one moves on to more specific moral norms and concrete moral judgments, there is more room for failures both as to the knowledge of a moral norm and with respect to how generally the norm holds. (For example, borrowed goods should usually be returned, but if someone whom one knows to be planning a terrorist attack asks for a borrowed weapon to be returned, one might be justified in refusing to return it. In such cases, there may be exceptions to general norms.[10])

The first principles of practical reason state self-evident practical propositions,[11] and the most common moral precepts (which roughly correspond to the right hand table of the Decalogue) are generally known to all, because they are conclusions following closely from the first principles. Human beings move from these general principles to specific moral judgments in various ways.

Some human actions are so evidently good or bad that after very little reflection one is able reasonably to approve or disapprove of them, whereas other actions cannot finally be judged morally good or bad without much careful deliberation, including, ordinarily, consideration of the circumstances. The greater the complexity of the matter, the more difficult the judgment. And, obviously, not all persons are equally competent to deliberate carefully when it comes to the most difficult matters. Some matters, as Aquinas suggested, are evident (or, indeed, self-evident) "only to the wise."[12]

To recapitulate the view held by natural law theorists: basic moral norms are widely known, though in some cases they or their more specific applications may be obscured by wayward passions or corrupt customs or habits. The movement from basic principles to concrete judgments, however, will vary according to the complexity of a given case, and the more complex the case, the more wisdom is required to make the appropriate judgment. (In Macedo's terms, the more complex the issues, the larger the "gap" between first principles and actual moral norms.)

It is particularly important for our purposes to note that knowledge of the moral precepts of the natural law, even the more general ones, does not necessarily imply the ability to construct effective arguments explaining moral norms and their application. Most ordinary people cannot construct sophisticated moral arguments, but, at least according to natural law theorists, they have a grasp of the most basic moral norms. That is to say, it is possible for many or even most people to know that a certain act (e.g., rape, shoplifting, income tax evasion) is wrong, but not necessarily to be able to articulate and defend that knowledge very well.

Take a simple example. Murder is wrong. Few people object to that proposition. They know it to be true. If you want to have some fun, however, simply play devil's advocate for the contrary proposition with a group of students and observe their (usually lame) efforts to "prove" that murder is wrong. Their inability to articulate a well-reasoned argument does not mean that they are wrong about murder or even that their belief that murder is wrong does not really amount to knowledge; it suggests, rather, that there is a difference between "articulate" and "inarticulate" knowledge. We suspect that a high proportion of the moral knowledge possessed by any of us is more or less inarticulate—and none the worse for that.[13]

Now the question that must be posed is this: when advocates of the public reason doctrine contend that liberalism requires reasoned arguments that are or can be "widely accepted," ones that "should be acceptable to everyone concerned," is it sufficient that these arguments be "acceptable" to people on the basis of what we have called "inarticulate knowledge"? If the answer is "no"—that is, if more developed and articulate knowledge is required—then the liberal public reason doctrine is utopian, at best. As such, it is simply unfit to govern political affairs in a world inhabited by actual human beings. If, however, the answer is "yes"—that is, if arguments can be considered publicly accessible even if they can be widely accepted only on the basis of inarticulate knowledge—then, contrary to what Macedo supposes, natural law arguments meet the standard of public accessibility.

Note, too, that if a realistic standard is adopted—i.e., a standard that admits inarticulate knowledge—Macedo's simple distinction between natural law teachings that are "too complex" to be publicly accessible, on the one hand, and mere "popular prejudices" about how human beings should behave, on the other, tends to break down. What are from the liberal viewpoint mere "popular prejudices" may or may not truly be prejudices. If the liberal view of sexual morality is wrong, for example, as most natural law theorists believe it to be, then opposition to homosexual and other nonmarital sex acts may be based on moral insight, not mere prejudice. And the insight may constitute not only the "articulate knowledge" of philosophically trained natural law theorists, but also the "inarticulate knowledge" of ordinary people who are not adept at constructing philosophical arguments. The view of ordinary people about the wrongness of nonmarital sexual conduct may be no more a "prejudice" than their view about the wrongness of murder.

Slavery and Abortion

It is also worth considering the possibility that what are truly prejudices can masquerade as rational judgments. As a result of corrupt customs, self-interest, and other factors, mere prejudices can become widely shared in a society or within a segment of a society, including a society's most elite segment. And where prejudices are widely shared by an elite, they may receive the most sophisticated (albeit, in the end, specious) rational defenses from influential intellectuals and other highly regarded figures. We think that these considerations highlight a particular difficulty in all efforts known to us to establish a plausible doctrine of liberal public reason. To expose this difficulty, let us reflect as Macedo has done, on a moral issue that was once debated by apparently reasonable people of goodwill, but on which we now have a moral consensus, namely, slavery.

In his contribution to the current volume, Macedo strives mightily to differentiate slavery, which was once, but is no longer, a subject of intense moral controversy, from abortion, which, of course, is such a subject today. For the moment, let us put aside questions about public reason with respect to the religious foundations of much abolitionist thinking and activity. We want simply to ask this question: Does Macedo give us any reason to believe that the arguments against slavery and the arguments against abortion are essentially different, in that one of them (the antislavery argument) meets the demands of public reason and the other (the anti-abortion argument) does not? We think that the answer to that question is no.

Macedo's position is that abortion comes "down to a fairly close call between two well-reasoned sets of arguments" and therefore "the best thing for reasonable people to do might be to acknowledge the difficulty of the argument and the burdens of reason, to respect their opponents, and to compromise with them, and to find some middle ground that gives something to each side while the argument goes forward."[14] Macedo explicitly rejects arguments by John Finnis and Robert George that abortion is not usually even a close call.[15] Crucially, he denies George's claim that the development from zygote to adulthood occurs without "substantial change."[16] He simply asserts, without argument, that it is "unreasonable to deny that there are also grounds for ascribing substantial moral weight to the development of basic neural or brain functions—the development of sensory capacity, consciousness, or sentience—and viability."[17]

Our main concern here is not the correctness *vel non* of Macedo's argument about abortion, so the following section is something of a digression, but it is one that we cannot omit. Macedo misunderstands George's argument in a profoundly important respect, and fails to come to grips with it in another. First, he takes George's reference to "substantial change" to mean "a lot of change," when in fact George's point, which is scientifically and philosophically incontestable, is that there is no *essential* change or change of natures. The development of a human being from the zygotic stage of its existence to the adult stage is the development of a distinct, unitary substance. At no point in its development was the human being that is now an adult a different substance, being, or thing than he or she is currently. Using the phrase in its accepted philosophical sense, that is precisely what George means in saying that there is no "substantial change." At every stage of its existence—from zygote to adult—the human individual remains the same self-integrating human organism, an organism which, given a hospitable environment, develops itself and directs its own integral organic functioning.

To be sure, the human individual develops and changes in many ways—with respect to basic neural or brain functions, for example, or becoming viable outside the womb—but those changes never involve a change from its being one sort of thing (or, in philosophical terms, "substance") to its being another, much as occurs when sperm and egg unite and those two things become one new essentially (or "substantially") different thing.

Macedo does not really *argue* that it is "unreasonable to deny that there are also grounds for ascribing substantial moral weight" to certain developments (neural or brain functions, viability), he just asserts it. George's principle is simple and straightforward: the being in the womb is a human being, the same human being from conception onward. As a human being, it shares with other human beings certain fundamental rights, including a right not to be killed. If there are reasonable grounds for saying that more developed human beings should not be killed, but that human beings at an earlier stage of development can be killed, then Macedo ought to give them. But, frankly, we doubt that any argument about human rights that turns, for example, on lung capacity—as the viability argument does—will meet the most minimal standards of reason or public accessibility.

This is not to say, of course, that the proponents of a right to take unborn human life have no legitimate concerns on their side. And therefore, as Macedo argues, "the best thing may be to try to give something to both sides,"[18] to find some middle ground. But, contrary to what Macedo argues, *Planned Parenthood v. Casey* is not the middle ground, since it attends to the innocence and right to life of the unborn child hardly at all.[19] Consider the following as a proper middle ground: prohibiting abortion, in order to give fair weight to the unborn child's right to life; providing assistance (financial, medical, emotional) to women with difficult pregnancies, in order to minimize the costs of carrying through such pregnancies; promoting laws that make adoption easier, to provide for children whose biological parents are unable or unwilling to care for them (and to minimize the long-term costs of carrying an unborn child to full term); educating people (especially young people) to the enormous costs (especially human costs) of irresponsible sexual activity and also to the equal responsibility of men for the children they participate in conceiving; and focusing penalties for abortion not on pregnant women, but on those who perform abortions.

Now some people probably will find the assertion that this is a "middle position" outrageous. They will say that it simply represents the position embraced by the pro-life movement in this country, and on that point they would, of course, be right. This experience of outrage may be useful, however, if it gives them some inkling of how their opponents feel when *Casey*, and a variety of other recent, much ballyhooed "compromises," are described as a "middle ground" in this debate.[20]

But let us return to the central question of this paper, namely, the liberal doctrine of public reason. We have considered Macedo's position on how the public reason doctrine applies to abortion. What is his position on its application to slavery? The question arises, of course, because of the many striking similarities between abolitionist and pro-life causes and movements and the public controversies surrounding them. Macedo says that "there is something a little slick in drawing quick analogies between slavery and abortion in order to impugn public reason,"[21] but he does not explain why. If morally principled antiabortion arguments fail to meet the test of public reason today, would similarly morally principled antislavery arguments have somehow met the test of public reason in the 1850's? We think the answer has to be no. Here is what Macedo says on the point:

> Projecting myself back to, say, 1857, it seems quite doubtful to me that the merits of the arguments for slavery would have appeared in as reasonable a light as do both sides in today's abortion debate. . . . I suppose there were some whose defense of slavery, coupled perhaps with opposition to "wage slavery" in the North, amounted to a reasoned public case, worthy of some sort of respect.[22]

He then goes on to deny that this situation called for principled compromise, citing George's argument that "respect may sometimes be owed to persons who in general exhibit reasonableness and good will, but not to some position they have adopted, which one regards as so deeply misguided and wrong as to be unworthy of respect."[23]

The difference between abortion and slavery, as Macedo views the matter, then, is simple: he thinks that both sides of the abortion debate really have reasons (so a "principled compromise" such as *Casey*—which, on its own terms, reaffirms "the central holding" of *Roe v. Wade*[24]—is appropriate), whereas even decent people who supported the slavery position had no reasons, but were merely the victims of their own prejudices and corrupt traditions (so public reason would not have required some sort of principled compromise, such as Stephen Douglas's proposal to leave slavery to individual states and territories, perhaps). The problem, of course, is that there were many Americans—even decent ones—who believed that slavery was just and good for everyone concerned, and there are many people today (ourselves among them) who believe that the pro-abortion rights position Macedo finds reasonable is "so deeply misguided and wrong as to be unworthy of respect," even though people of general reasonableness who happen to hold that position should be respected.

So where has the requirement of meeting conditions of public reason gotten us? Nowhere very useful.[25]

Public Reason as Argumentative Sleight-of-Hand

In the case of *Trimble v. Gordon* (1977), then-Justice William Rehnquist wrote an interesting opinion analyzing the judicial use of the Equal Protection Clause. Rehnquist argued that the prevailing equal protection doctrine authorized such broad second-guessing of legislative decisions that it could be viewed "as a cat-o'-nine-tails to be kept in the judicial closet as a threat to legislatures which may, in the view of judges, get out of hand and pass 'arbitrary', 'illogical', or 'unreasonable' laws."[26]

Public reason is a similar "cat-o'-nine-tails." A good example of this can be found, we think, in Macedo's debate with Robert George, Gerard Bradley, and Hadley Arkes on the issue of homosexuality.[27] Macedo's original position on natural law theory, in *Liberal Virtues*, as we saw above, was that it failed to meet the requirements of public justification. But later, in a book chapter responding to John Finnis's defense of public authority to discourage homosexual conduct (within the limits of the subsidiarity principle), he seemed to change directions somewhat. In his conclusion, Macedo argued that

> [t]he best way of thinking about political power in a democratic constitutionalist regime such as ours is as the shared property of reasonable citizens, who should be able to offer one another reasons that can publicly be seen as good to justify the use of that power. Many natural law arguments (including those discussed above [i.e., Finnis's arguments about homosexual acts]) are indeed acceptably public, as Finnis asserts: the reason and evidence on which they are based are not overly complex or vague, and they can be shared openly with fellow citizens. The vice of the new natural law position described above is not its vagueness, complexity, or lack of public

accessibility but, as we saw, its unreasonable narrowness and arbitrary extension.[28]

It is worth noting that Finnis' arguments in his paper were not the stuff of everyday conversation. If not "overly complex or vague," they were still arguments requiring some measure of learning and a high degree of intellectual ability.

Macedo then extended his critique of contemporary natural law thinking on homosexuality in a *Georgetown Law Journal* article, to which George and Bradley (and, separately, Arkes) responded at length.[29] In Macedo's article there is some ambivalence about the relationship between conservative moral arguments and public reason. In a footnote early in the argument, he says that

> [t]here may be something appropriate about the limited depth in which we can consider the new natural law arguments. As Rawls has recently argued, the reasons offered for justifying and shaping our basic rights and liberties ought to be ones whose force can be appreciated by people lacking specialized intellectual sophistication and by people proceeding from a variety of abstract, not unreasonable, philosophical assumptions.[30]

There is also a somewhat ambiguous reference to public reasonableness at the end of the article. It is ambiguous, because moral arguments advanced by natural law thinkers and other "conservatives" are said to fail the test of public reasonableness, but the ground for the failure seems to be that they are simply not reasonable arguments, rather than that they are overly complex and inaccessible to ordinary citizens.[31]

As we indicated above, Macedo's argument drew a very lengthy response from George and Bradley. Macedo's subsequent reply argued both that their response was not adequate philosophically and also that

> it now seems to me even clearer, moreover, that insofar as it is not possible to defend the value of some homosexual relationships in natural law terms, this is true for reasons that are neither understood

nor accepted by the vast majority of the public. These reasons are too open to reasonable disagreement to furnish a basis for demarcating fundamental rights and liberties in a regime properly dedicated to the authority of public reason.[32]

Macedo repeats this argument in his concluding remarks on George and Bradley's response:

> If our disagreements indeed lie in these difficult philosophical quarrels, about which reasonable people have long disagreed, then our differences lie precisely in the territory that John Rawls rightly (on my view) marks off as inappropriate to the fashioning of our basic rights and liberties. It is . . . inappropriate to deny people fundamental aspects of equality based on reasons and arguments whose force can only be appreciated by those who accept difficult to assess claims about the nature and incommensurability of basic goods, the relationship between intrinsic and instrumental value, and the dispute over whether pleasure is a reason for action. I submit that if the new natural law does not fail for the fairly straightforward reasons I have offered . . . then the new natural law argument fails as a basis for fashioning basic liberties and the principles of equality on grounds of its esotericism.[33]

So Macedo, at this point, has come full circle, back to his original position that natural law is unable to meet the demands of public justification.

Macedo is apparently trying to establish a "Catch-22" situation for natural law theorists. If they do not put forward a powerful and intellectually sophisticated argument for their positions regarding political life and moral issues, then they fail the requirement of reason per se. Their positions become nothing more than the popular prejudices, the "unreasoned populism" criticized in *Liberal Virtues*. If, on the other hand, natural law theorists do provide powerful and intellectually sophisticated reasons for their positions, then ipso facto they are going beyond the limits of public justification, because their arguments become too complicated and controversial. "Public reason" is serving as that ever-convenient cat-o'-nine-tails that can be dragged out as soon as the argumentative going gets tough. In fact, the more sophisticated the natural law argument, the easier it becomes to dismiss it for not being "publicly accessible"! Yet in his article in the current volume, Macedo asks, in regard to Michael Sandel: "Or is Sandel just [incorrectly] supposing that the sort of moral arguments with respect to nuclear deterrence offered by the Catholic bishops, or *natural law arguments on homosexuality*, are in some basic way at odds with public reasonableness?"[34] So, it appears, natural law arguments regarding homosexuality are now back in the other column: legitimate, from the standpoint of public reasonableness (whatever their truth value otherwise).

Whatever Macedo's final stance on the relation of natural law arguments against homosexual conduct, for example, and public reasonableness, so many shifts and such inconsistency in the argument of an impeccably honest and highly sophisticated advocate of the liberal public reason doctrine itself suggests that something must be wrong with the doctrine.

Note also how Macedo's line of argument exemplifies an enduring and characteristic feature of liberal argumentation. "Equality" (between, e.g., what law and moral tradition have long understood to be marital intercourse, on the one hand, and sodomitical relations—heterosexual or homosexual—on the other) is assumed to be the undifferentiated "default" position for society; it doesn't require being established by an argument, and it's nothing if it's not simple. Having arbitrarily established this as the starting point, the burden of proof is placed on the opponents of liberalism to justify any departure from the liberal conception of equality, and if they don't come up with a *compelling* but *simple* response, the liberal position wins. But this is not much more than playing a game with loaded dice.[35]

If, on the other hand, advocates of homosexual rights and other liberal ideas about sexuality, for example, were subject to the same requirement of establishing a satisfactory philosophical basis for their position—and if their simple assertions of a right to engage in sodomitical acts or a right of same-sex couples to obtain marriage licenses were dismissed just as easily as conservative positions on the grounds that they reflect mere "prejudices," undisciplined desires, or special pleading—then their arguments would quickly have to become more sophisticated, and thereby become "inaccessible" to "people lacking specialized intellectual sophistication"[36].

Public Reason and Religion

There is much that might be said about liberal public reason and religion, though we do not have the space to explore the question very far here. Let us take this occasion simply to mention a few problems.

By emphasizing the "reason" of public reason, liberals can significantly circumscribe the role that religion plays in public discourse, at least insofar as religion is considered to be nonrational. And the "public" part of public reason can further this process insofar as religion is understood as essentially a set of beliefs based on claims to private revelation. Rawls and Macedo both adopt this general approach at various points in their writing. But both elements of the approach are problematic. Religion claims, in at least some forms, or at least up to some point, to be rational; moreover, it typically proposes that the revelation to which it responds is in the most important respects fully publicly accessible.

To take one example from current controversies, let us consider euthanasia. There are various reasons for opposing euthanasia on moral grounds, and we suppose that some of these might pass muster before the bar of liberal public reason. But let us consider a straightforward theological ground for opposing euthanasia, and ask whether it meets the requirements of public reason.

> But though this be a State of Liberty, yet it is not a State of Licence, though Man in that State have an uncontrollable Liberty, to dispose of his Person or Possessions, yet he has not Liberty to destroy

himself, or so much as any Creature in his Possession, but where some nobler use, than its bare Preservation calls for it. The State of Nature has a Law of Nature to govern it, which obliges everyone: And Reason, which is that Law, teaches all Mankind, who will but consult it, that being all equal and independent, no one ought to harm another in his Life, Health, Liberty, or Possessions. For Men being all the Workmanship of one Omnipotent, and infinitely wise Maker; All the Servants of one Sovereign Master, sent into the World by his order and about his business, they are his Property, whose Workmanship they are, made to last during his, not one anothers Pleasure.[37]

This argument comes, of course, from "the greatest liberal of them all"[38], John Locke. Is it compatible with public reason?

Before 1947 and *Everson v. Board of Education*[39], it is fair to say that American public philosophy took the political relevance of a providential God for granted. Perhaps the greatest testimony to this was the publicly declared judgment that men's inalienable rights, the protection of which was government's supreme purpose, rested on a (natural) theological foundation: "We hold these truths to be self-evident, that all men are created equal, that they are endowed by their Creator with certain unalienable rights . . ." This was, presumably, the foundation for Justice Douglas's famous statement in *Zorach v. Clauson* that "[w]e are a religious people whose institutions presuppose a Supreme Being."[40] Beginning with *Everson*, however, "separation of church and state" has been gradually, but radically, redefined to view public acknowledgment of God as a violation of fundamental constitutional principles. This has primarily been the work of intellectuals and their allies in the "knowledge class," whose religious beliefs and practices, it should be noted, are in most cases dramatically out of line with the beliefs and practices of their fellow citizens.

In this area, as in the area of morality, we would argue that one must distinguish between different levels of knowledge: "inarticulate knowledge" and more fully developed knowledge. Most

Americans believe in God, though few could get very far with, say, an unbelieving professor from their state university in arguing on the subject. We would nonetheless contend that they possess genuine knowledge. Their views are, to be sure, less sophisticated than the views of professional academics or other intellectuals, but they possess the considerable virtue of being true. Is the existence of a providential God (e.g., a God who creates and attends to his Creation), therefore, "publicly accessible" and thus defensible at the bar of public reason (broadly and properly defined—not Rawlsian public reason)? We, like virtually all the founders of American government, think it is.

Some religious believers (perhaps especially certain evangelicals) might go further. They appeal to the Bible, and argue that the Bible is true, and should be recognized as true by any reasonable person. To the extent that "faith" is necessary, they would argue that faith is available to all. (They make no gnostic claim to a body of special, secret knowledge, accessible only to an elite.) And such believers are nothing if not willing to share their "reasons" in public! On what nontheological grounds can liberals deny that such claims are, in fact, "publicly accessible" to all? The simple fact that "some people don't believe" won't do; that's true of virtually all positions (certainly including liberal contentions). Unless "reason," as liberals understand it and its implications, is said to be, in principle, a superior source of knowledge, why should liberal reason be privileged over evangelical faith? In a given society, faith might actually be viewed by a large majority of society as a more, rather than less, "publicly accessible" form of knowledge. Aside from comprehensive liberalism's religious scepticism, is there a clear reason, other than the conventional beliefs of American intellectual class, why religion—even in the form of revealed religion—should be considered any less publicly accessible than, say, Rawlsian liberalism?

We do not deny that religious differences—especially those based on differing views of divine revelation—can make for considerable tensions in the public sphere, and that prudence dictates that the fact of religious pluralism be taken seriously into account in determining the appropriate character of social discourse and deliberation. In the absence of a more extensive discussion of that complex issue, let us only say for the moment that we see no reason to believe that liberal public reason will prove itself to be more helpful a concept when considering the relation of religion and politics than it is when considering the relation of politics and morality.

Conclusion

These observations indicate that liberal public reason is ultimately implausible and, in any event, an intellectually unhelpful doctrine. Its measures are unclear. It is difficult to square with the complexities of human knowledge. It is easily susceptible to partisan manipulation, especially by comprehensive liberals whose partisan interests, after all, it almost always serves. On the whole, we would be better off without it.

The alternative, we suggest, is to expand the concept to a genuine, broad—i.e., not arbitrarily truncated—idea of public reason. That would be welcome to natural law theorists, who are happy to contend on that level playing field in the struggle to identify and embody in law and public policy truths available to rational inquiry, understanding, and judgment.

Notes

1. Stephen Macedo, *Liberal Virtues*. Oxford, UK: Clarendon Press, 1990.
2. The main difference between Rawls and Macedo is that Macedo is much more definite—and unapologetic—about political liberalism's fostering of a particular way of life that is incompatible with other ways of life. Public policy, moreover, can fairly attend to fostering the essential prerequisites of this way of life. At points, therefore, we think that Macedo may cross the line into a form of comprehensive

liberalism, though he would probably deny this. See *Liberal Virtues*, pp. 59–64.

3. Macedo, *Liberal Virtues*, p. 12.

4. Ibid., pp. 63–64.

5. Ibid., p. 47.

6. Ibid., p. 211.

7. Ibid., p. 212.

8. *Summa Theologica* I–II, Q. 94, a. 4: "It is therefore evident that, as regards the general principles whether of speculative or of practical reason, truth or rectitude is the same for all, and is equally known by all." Qualified in Q. 94, a. 6: "As to those general precepts, the natural law, in the abstract, can nowise be blotted out from men's hearts. But it is blotted out in the case of a particular action, in so far as reason is hindered from applying the general principle to a particular point of practice, on account of concupiscence or some other passion."

9. *Summa Theologica* I–II, Q. 94, a. 4. ". . . the natural law, as to general principles, is the same for all, both as to rectitude and as to knowledge. But as to certain matters of detail, which are conclusions, as it were, of those general principles, it is the same for all in the majority of cases, both as to rectitude and as to knowledge; and yet in some few cases it may fail, both as to rectitude . . . and as to knowledge, since in some the reason is perverted by passion, or evil habit, or an evil disposition of nature; thus formerly theft, although it is expressly contrary to the natural law, was not considered wrong among the Germans, as Julius Caesar relates . . ."

10. Ibid.

11. On the (much misunderstood) meaning of "self-evidence" as natural law theorists use the term in relation to the most basic principles of practical thinking, see Robert P. George, "Recent Criticism of Natural Law Theory," *University of Chicago Law Review*, 55 (1988), 1386–89.

12. "Some matters connected with human actions are so evident, that after very little consideration one is able at once to approve or disapprove of them by means of these general first principles; while some matters cannot be the subject of judgment without much consideration of the various circumstances, which all are not compe-

tent to do carefully, but only those who are wise." *Summa Theologica* I–II, Q. 100, a. 1.

13. For a clear and, we think, decisive answer to Macedo's claim that moral norms as understood by natural law theorists are beyond the capacities for understanding of "most people," and therefore not legitimate grounds for legislation, see John Finnis, "Is Natural Law Theory Compatible with Limited Government?" in *Natural Law, Liberalism, and Morality,* ed. Robert P. George. Oxford, UK: Clarendon Press, 1996, pp. 1–26, esp. 10–11.

14. Macedo, p. 29 of this volume.

15. Finnis, "Is Natural Law Theory Compatible with Limited Government?" in *Natural Law, Liberalism, and Morality*; George, "Public Reason and Political Conflict: Abortion and Homosexuality," *Yale Law Journal* 106 (1997), 2475.

16. George, "Public Reason and Political Conflict," p. 2493.

17. Macedo, p. 32 of this volume.

18. Ibid.

19. 120 L.Ed.2d 674 (1992).

20. See, for example, Eileen McConaugh, *Breaking the Abortion Deadlock: From Choice to Consent.* New York: Oxford University Press, 1996, and Roger Rosenblatt, "How to End the Abortion War," *The New York Times Magazine,* 141 (Jan. 19, 1992), p. 26.

21. Macedo, p. 42 of this volume.

22. Ibid.

23. Ibid.

24. 120 L.Ed.2d 674, p. 699.

25. Rawls, in "The Idea of Public Reason Revisited," *University of Chicago Law Review,* 64 (1997), 802, contends that it is a "misunderstanding" that "an argument in public reason could not side with Lincoln against Douglas in their debates of 1858. He simply asserts that "[s]ince the rejection of slavery is a clear case of securing the constitutional essential of the equal basic liberties, surely Lincoln's view was reasonable (even if not the most reasonable), while Douglas's was not" (ibid.). But, of course, whether blacks were fully human beings and appropriate subjects of "equal basic liberties" was precisely the point of contention in the slavery debate of that time, as it is the point of contention, in our time, regarding very young

human beings still in the womb. Rawls is right about Lincoln and the rights of blacks, of course, in just the same way as those who seek to protect the rights of the unborn today.

26. 430 U.S. 777 (1977).
27. Stephen Macedo, "Homosexuality and the Conservative Mind" and "Reply to Critics," *Georgetown Law Journal*, 84 (December 1995), 261–300 and 329–38. See also the Finnis-Macedo exchange on the same subject in George, ed. *Natural Law, Liberalism, and Morality.*
28. Stephen Macedo, "Against the Old Sexual Morality and the New Natural Law," in George, ed. *Natural Law, Liberalism, and Morality,* p. 44.
29. It is characteristic of Macedo's intellectual integrity and fair mindedness that he personally encouraged the editors of the *Georgetown Law Journal* to solicit essays critical of his views on homosexuality for publication in response to his article.
30. Macedo, "Homosexuality and the Conservative Mind," p. 264, n. 15.
31. Ibid., p. 299.
32. Macedo, "Reply to Critics," p. 329.
33. Ibid., p. 335.
34. Macedo, p. 36 of this volume (emphasis added).
35. Again this strikes us as a recurring feature of much liberal argumentation. One of us noted the same mode of argument in Bruce Ackerman's *Social Justice and the Liberal State* in a review written over fifteen years ago. See Christopher Wolfe, "Liberal Foundations for Liberalism?" in *The Public Interest,* 62 (winter 1981), 127–28. Although it is less clear in the earlier discussion of abortion, we think that the same principle operates there. The burden of proof is placed on anti-abortion advocates to prove that life begins at conception and that such life is entitled to all the normal protection accorded at least to innocent human life. The battle rages, with arguments put forth on both sides, and then a draw is declared, and a "moderate compromise" that reaffirms abortion rights is put forward as the appropriate resolution.

Complex moral argumentation is always considered to be inconclusive, and as "ties go to the runner" in baseball umpiring, the resultant "ties" on civil liberties issues always go to the side favoring more "freedom," which is assumed to be the liberal position. This approach is particularly questionable in a democracy, since it usually involves judicial overruling of legislative enactments, despite the "antimajoritarian problem" implicit in that disposition. In a democratic republic, one would think that "ties" ought to result in upholding legislative acts.

36. In this regard, note particularly Macedo's own efforts to prevent his rejection of natural law norms regarding sexuality from becoming a defense of promiscuity. (Macedo, "Homosexuality and the Conservative Mind," p. 261). Even apart from the question of whether Macedo makes an adequate intellectual case against promiscuity (which we doubt; a case merely for moderation doesn't rule out anything other than "immoderate promiscuity"), it seems likely that the same kinds of objections Macedo uses against the accessibility of natural law arguments can be used against his own arguments.

37. John Locke, *Two Treatises of Government,* ed. Peter Laslett. New York: Mentor, 1965, p. 311.

38. Stephen Macedo, "Multiculturalism for the religious right? Defending liberal civic education," *Journal of Philosophy of Education,* 29 (1995), 231.

39. 330 U.S. 1 (1947).

40. 343 U.S. 306, 313 (1952).

John Finnis

Abortion, Natural Law, and Public Reason

Public Reason and the "Right to Kill the Unborn"

The issue I was asked to debate with Professor Reiman was: Is the abortion question the kind of question that should be publicly regulated, or should it be outside the public sphere in a liberal society, on the grounds, for example, that it is not amenable to "public reason"? As Reiman will I'm sure agree, the issue thus framed for debate between us is scarcely debatable. Will anyone argue that abortion should be left to private judgment, so that people who judge it as homicide are entitled to use force to prevent their fellow citizens engaging in it (just as they are entitled to use force to prevent infanticide or sexual intercourse between adults and eight-year-old boys)? Every society, liberal or illiberal, takes a public stand on the question of whether abortion is or is not a form of criminal activity.

The need for the law and public policy to take such a stand has become more and more obvious, for two reasons. The first has to do with the standard purpose of abortion, as that term is commonly used: to end the life of a fetus/unborn child. As Reiman argues,[1] the right to abortion that he is interested in defending, and that many others are interested in having, is a right that would be *negated* if it were reduced to "[a woman's] right to expel an unwelcome fetus from her body, and only to end its life if necessary for the expulsion."[2] The right that Reiman and so many others defend is the right precisely to kill the unwelcome fetus. The significance of this is made clear by the second reason: unborn children who are welcome and thought to be in danger can now be the beneficiaries of elaborate therapeutic attentions. From a month or so after conception, their condition, their individual appearance and characteristics, and their every movement can be followed on the ultrasound screen almost as clearly as a close-up real-time film of (say) Professor Reiman working at his desk. Their medical problems can be and very frequently are attended to in much the same ways as after their birth. Medical practitioners engaged in such activities routinely say and think that they have two patients.[3] And it is obvious to everyone that any medical practitioners who took advantage of this sort of opportunity to kill the unborn child (without the request of the mother), pursuant to some private policy of (say) killing Jews or the children of atheists, would be ethically and legally liable to some plausible charge of homicide or something savoring of homicide.[4] Since the difference between the unborn, the partially born, and the newborn is now known to be, for practical purposes, no more (and no less) than the difference between being (wholly or partly) inside and outside the mother's body, any society, liberal or not, must and will publicly regulate the ways in which medical practitioners and others deal with the unborn (or partially born), particularly those dealings that by intention or negligence result in the death of the unborn (or partially unborn).

"Public Reason" and Political Theory's Central Tradition

Have we, then, something to debate, other than the straightforward question of what form the public regulation of abortion—killing the unborn with intent to kill—should take? Well, we were given not only an alleged issue, but also a title: "Abortion, Natural Law, and Public Reason." The term "public reason" has recently been introduced into political theoretical discourse by John Rawls, and, as it happened, he chose to illustrate his use of the term by reference to the issue of the regulation of abortion. So perhaps there is something here for Professor Reiman and me to debate. Unfortunately, Rawls's remarks about abortion do not, perhaps, show his work to best advantage. But it will be valuable to explore the question of whether "public reason" is a concept or nest of concepts worth adopting into political theory, using abortion as a test case whenever our exploration would be advanced by carrying out a test.

I should say at the outset that the attractions of the term "public reason" have not been much diminished for me by the discovery that Rawls's own usage is (as almost everyone agrees) confused and arbitrary. "Public reason" seems to me quite a good phrase for summarily conveying the gist of at least four features of classical political thought as expounded by (say) Thomas Aquinas:[5]

(1) The proper function of the state's law and government is limited. In particular, its role is not (as Aristotle had supposed) to make people integrally good but only to maintain peace and justice in interpersonal relationships.[6] In this respect, the public realm, the *respublica*, is different from certain other associations such as family and church, associations which, albeit with limited means, can properly aspire to bring it about that their members become integrally good people. As Rawls says, "public reason" is contrasted not with "private reason"—"there is no such thing as private reason"[7]— but with the ways of deliberating appropriate to all nonpublic associations, i.e., all associations other than the political community.[8] The deliberations of the political community as such—that is, of its rulers, including voters, as such—proceed in the appropriate way only if they are concerned to determine those requirements of justice and peace which Aquinas regularly names "public good."[9]

(2) In determining and enforcing the requirements of public good, the state's lawmakers and other rulers (including voters) are entitled to impose as requirements only those practical principles

which are accessible to all people whatever their religious beliefs or cultural practices. These are the principles (*communia principia rationis practicae*)[10] which, together with their entailments[11] are called in the tradition "natural law," on the understanding that they are "natural" because, *and only because*[12] they are rational—requirements of being practically reasonable—and thus accessible to beings whose nature includes rational capacities.

(3) The central case of government is the rule of a free people, and the central case of law is coordination of willing subjects by law which, by its fully public character (promulgation),[13] its clarity,[14] generality,[15] stability,[16] and practicability,[17] treats them as partners in public reason.[18]

(4) "Any activity is to be pursued in a way appropriate to its purpose. . . . One sort of academic disputation is designed to remove doubts about *whether* such-and-such is so. In disputations of this sort you should above all use authorities acceptable to those with whom you are disputing . . . *And if you are disputing with people who accept no authority, you must resort to natural reasons.*"[19]

"Public Reason" and Rawls

The central tenet of Rawls's construct "Political Liberalism" in his book *Political Liberalism* is "the liberal principle of legitimacy": political questions which concern or border on constitutional essentials or basic questions of justice will be settled fully properly only if settled by principles and ideals that all citizens "may reasonably be expected to endorse." Rawls terms such principles and ideals "public reason(s) and [public] justification." The whole point of the principle of legitimacy is to rule out as illegitimate, in a certain context, certain principles and ideals and in general *theses*, even though they are or may well be true—i.e., to rule them out on grounds completely distinct from their falsity[20] or their unreasonableness, judged comprehensively.[21]

Rawls's formulations of the legitimacy principle are baffingly ambiguous. When one says of a thesis, "all may reasonably be expected to endorse it," is one predicting the behavior of people or assessing the rational strength of the thesis? Does one mean that reasonable observers will agree that all citizens *will* (or at least *are likely to*) endorse it? Or does one make a judgment about the grounds, evidence or reasons for and against the thesis and thus about the (un)reasonableness of anyone who refuses to endorse it?

There is evidence in favor of the predictive, external-viewpoint reading. For example, Rawls says of a particular thesis that even though it may be true, "reasonable persons *are bound to* differ uncompromisingly" about it.[22] The phrase "are bound to" seems on the whole to be in the predictive mode, not the mode of speech of someone assessing the thesis itself as reasonable or unreasonable.[23]

But the external-viewpoint interpretation leads to a particularly gross form of veto, by majorities or indeed by minorities. So it is not too surprising that there is also plenty of textual evidence in favor of a normative, internal viewpoint on Rawls's own legitimacy principle, such that the phrase "can reasonably be expected to endorse thesis X" is to be read as signifying a judgment on the sorts of grounds there are for endorsing or denying thesis X.[24] Particularly interesting is the passage in which Rawls finally faces up to "rationalist believers" in a "comprehensive religious or philosophical doctrine" who "contend that their beliefs are open to and can be fully established by reason" and are "so fundamental that to insure their being rightly settled justifies civil strife." Having curiously suggested that this view is uncommon, when actually it is (in some form) the claim of the entire central tradition of natural law theory in philosophy and theology, Rawls interprets the rationalist believers' claim as a denial of "what we have called 'the fact of reasonable pluralism'". But their claim could not be a *denial* of that fact unless the "fact" of reasonable pluralism is in the same logical field as the rationalist believers' claim that their beliefs can be fully established by reason. And Rawls's recipe for dealing with the rationalist believers is to claim that they are "mistaken" in thinking that their beliefs can be "publicly and fully established by reason"—a claim that cannot reasonably be made by Rawls without looking, in what I have been calling an internal, normative way, at the merits of the rationalist believers' arguments as arguments.[25]

So much, then, for the radical ambiguity of Rawls's principle of legitimacy and thesis about public reason.[26] What are his grounds for putting it forward in any of its possible senses?

The principle of legitimacy and the limits or guidelines of public reason "have the same basis as the substantive principles of justice." That is, they would be adopted by the parties in the Original Position, because those parties would be failing their responsibility as trustees for the people who will live under the principles they adopt in the Original Position, unless they adopted the principle that the application of the substantive principles be "guided by judgment and inference, reasons and evidence that [those persons] can reasonably be expected to endorse."[27]

So the legitimacy thesis stands and falls with the "political constructivism" employed in his *A Theory of Justice* (1971). So it falls. That book rests on a fallacious or undefended claim. It proposes that we should recognize as principles of justice those, and only those, principles that would be adopted in a hypothetical Original Position, behind a "veil of ignorance," an artificial ignorance and risk-aversion supposed to be characteristic of the hypothetical parties who are to choose those principles of justice which will apply, outside the Original Position, in the real world. We can accept that principles that *would* be chosen in the Original Position would be equal and free from bias. But we cannot assume, as Rawls does, that principles that would not be chosen in the Original Position are therefore not principles of justice in the real world in which we may judge them without being hampered either by the Original Position's veil of ignorance about certain theoretical and practical truths, or by a degree of risk aversion which, if not unreasonable, is at best only one reasonable attitude amongst other, less-risk-averse attitudes.[28]

Political Liberalism is a vast elaboration—and perhaps to some extent is intended as a defense—of *A Theory of Justice*'s basic strategy and postulate of ignorance of value (i.e., thin theory of the good and "thick veil of ignorance"[29]), a device whose entire motivation is to ensure that (a) the Original Position construct will yield principles in line with Rawls's settled political opinions (what he calls the "acceptable conclusions" which a "model of practical reason" such as the Original Position must fit on pain of being revised or even abandoned altogether)[30], and (b) Rawls will not have to offer a defense of those opinions against the criticism that they ignore or contradict certain truths about human good.

Does *Political Liberalism* offer any satisfactory defense of the legitimacy principle's exclusion of "nonpublic" truths and reasons from one's public discussion and one's individual act of "voting on the most fundamental political questions"?

It seems not. No doubt a defense is intended in the remarks about "reasonable pluralism," the "ideal of democratic citizenship," and "civility." But all these simply assume what needs to be shown, that it is uncivil and undemocratic to propose to one's fellow citizens theses (on matters of fundamental justice) that one regards as true and established by evidence or reasons *available* to any reasonable person *willing to consider them* in an open-minded way.

Moreover, the legitimacy principle, as stated and understood by Rawls, is itself illegitimate, unreasonable, and uncivil. It is illegitimate because it censors truthful and reasonable public discourse and—worse—prohibits individual recourse to correct principles and criteria of practical judgment, in relation to fundamental political questions, without any coherent, principled reason for the prohibition. It is unreasonable because it restricts public deliberation and individual public action precisely on those matters where it is most important to be correct, i.e., where people's fundamental human rights are at stake, and above all where the question is *who* it is who has the fundamental rights our constitution and politics is concerned with; *who* are the persons for whose sake we have our law.[31]

Consider the example that Rawls himself brings forward to illustrate how his legitimacy principle works out in practice—his remarks about one of the very most important of the "fundamental political questions" currently debated, namely, abortion.[32] Here his legitimacy thesis makes him claim that one not only will be mistaken but will moreover be violating one's duties of democratic citizenship if one reasons in, e.g., the following way:

Every human being is entitled to an equal right to life;[33] unborn children, even in the first three months of their life, are human beings (as any medical textbook shows); therefore unborn children are entitled to the protection of the law against being deliberately killed even in the first three months of their life; and so I should vote for a law or constitutional amendment which recognizes that right.

Having asserted (by implication) that anyone who argues in such a way is not only mistaken but also antidemocratic (and, having explicitly claimed that such a person subscribes to a doctrine that is cruel and oppressive even if it allows exceptions for rape and incest), Rawls adds that any comprehensive doctrine that supports that reasoning "is to that extent unreasonable." So he asserts not merely that pro-life arguments on the abortion question are mistaken, but that they could not possibly be proper grounds for political action such as voting. And he claims to be able to say all this without inspecting the comprehensive doctrine(s) he condemns and without shouldering the responsibility of saying where the error in the reasoning about abortion lies. Instead of joining in the rational debate about abortion, he sidetracks and short-circuits it by simply declaring that "all reasonable people can be expected to agree" that healthy mature women have the right to kill a child during the first three months of his or her unborn life and probably for longer. So the legitimacy principle has an effect exactly opposite to what Rawls clearly intended. It generates a kind of incivility of its own, heat instead of light.

Rawls's legitimacy principle is a distorted and unwarranted analogue of a genuine principle of public reason, namely, that fundamental political, constitutional, and legal questions ought to be settled according to *natural right*, i.e., to principles and norms that are reasonable, using criteria of evidence and judgment that are accessible to all.[34] One reason he overlooks this alternative is that in thinking of the tradition, he clearly supposes that liberalism—in the first instance the comprehensive liberalism of Hume and Kant, and then his own "political" liberalism—differentiated itself from the tradition by adopting two views: (a) that knowledge of how we are to act is accessible to every person who is "normally reasonable and conscientious" *rather than* "only to some or to a few (the clergy, say)"; and (b) that the moral order required of us arises "in some way from human nature itself," say by reason, together with the requirements of our living together in society, *rather than* "from an external source, say from an order of values in God's intellect." He seems completely unaware that what I shall call *the tradition* in fact rejected these as false contrasts and so embraced precisely the positions he thinks characteristic of liberalism: (a) moral knowledge is available or accessible to all, and (b) moral knowledge arises in some way from human nature and reason and the requirements of social living.

Where the tradition parts company with Rawls is in relation to his "fact of reasonable pluralism/disagreement." When Rawls says "It is unrealistic—or worse, it arouses mutual suspicion and hostility—to suppose that all our differences are rooted solely in ignorance and perversity, or else in the rivalries for power, status, or economic gain," the tradition of natural law theorizing says, "Let's distinguish." There are many reasonable differences that arise from differences of sentiment, of prior commitment, and of belief about likely future outcomes. In such cases there is no uniquely correct opinion, though there are many incorrect opinions. But in relation to some matters, including at least some matters of basic rights, there are correct moral beliefs, accessible to all. In relation to such matters, differing opinions can only be rooted in ignorance or some subrational influence, and it is impossible to say that there is more than one "fully reasonable" or "perfectly reasonable" belief. If by *"perfectly reasonable though erroneous belief"* Rawls means a belief that is held without subjective moral fault in respect of the forming of it, I would say that that is an important category of *de facto* beliefs but one that would better be called, not "perfectly reasonable"—which it quite clearly is not—but "inculpably erroneous" or, in one traditional idiom, "invincibly ignorant." Public reasoning should be directed to overcoming the relevant mistakes, and public deliberations should be directed to avoiding them in practice, not preemptively surrendering to them.

Of course, a "liberalism of fear" is sometimes or even quite often warranted. It can often be morally reasonable to refrain from enforcing basic human rights, for example, for fear of provoking a war that one cannot win or that will impact unfairly, as most wars do, on the weakest.

The Rawlsian version of public reason is, as I said, particularly unreasonable because its demand—that moral truths and complicated ("elaborate") factual questions be excluded from public discourse and deliberation—is made *only* in relation to the most important questions of justice, such as whether it is acceptable to kill your unborn child at your choice, or acceptable to base our nation's defense policy on a plan to, under certain conditions, incinerate an enemy's civilian population with the side effect of poisoning half or more of the people of bystander nations. Such matters are apparently to be remitted to hunches or "judgments" untested by public political discourse about matters of principle or fact. That means they are remitted to the status quo established by sheer power of numbers or influence, a status quo—under-pinned by abortion on demand and anticivilian nuclear deterrence—with which Rawls happens, it seems, to be well satisfied "on balance."

Legitimacy, Bias, and the Rights of Children

Still, there is much to be said in favor of the underlying concern that gives both *A Theory of Justice* and *Political Liberalism* an initial plausibility and an appeal that survives the recognition that their central arguments are fallacious. That concern is the concern to avoid *bias*, unfairness between persons, violations of the Golden Rule. In the introduction to the paperback edition of *Political Liberalism,* Rawls gives a new prominence and a new formulation to a principle intended to give content to the demand that voting and other political determinations be made only by or on the basis of "public reasons."[35] This principle is the "criterion of reciprocity: our exercise of political power is proper only when we sincerely believe that the reasons we offer for our political action may reasonably be accepted by other citizens as a justification of those actions." It is the source of the liberal principle of legitimacy, and thus of the conception of public reason defended by Rawls. Its "role is to specify the nature of the political relation in a constitutional democratic regime as one of civic friendship." And it is itself the expression, or an immediate entailment, of the "intrinsic normative and moral ideal" without which "political liberalism" and Rawls's "political conception of justice" would fail to count as a moral conception at all (and thus would fail to be available to guide anyone's conscientious deliberations as a voter or other participant in governing). The ideal, Rawls says,

> can be set out in this way. Citizens are reasonable when, viewing one another as free and equal in a system of social co-operation *over generations,* they are prepared to offer one another fair terms of social co-operation (defined by principles and ideals) and they agree to act on those terms, *even at the cost of their own interests in particular situations,* provided that others accept those terms. For these terms to be fair terms, citizens offering them must reasonably think that those citizens to whom such terms are offered might also reasonably accept them. (emphases added)

This ideal, with its corresponding normative requirement, seems broadly reasonable. So we can ask how it bears on the situation of children.

Would it be consistent with justice, with civic friendship, with fairness and the criterion of reciprocity to adopt a scheme in which infants and children unwanted by their parents could be reared for the purposes of satisfying the desires of pedophiles by being raised up to the age of sexual desirability in circumstances (which would include the use of euphoric drugs) such that their eventual fate was entirely concealed from them, and on condition that after a sufficient period of use for sexual services they would be killed painlessly, without warning, while they slept? This is not a question of exegesis of Rawls's or anyone else's texts ("Does 'citizen' mean adult citizen?" "What does 'across generations' really mean?" "Are the parties to the criterion of reciprocity more narrowly defined than the parties to the Original Position?"). The question is one of substance, and the answer to it is clear enough.[36]

Rawls himself seems plainly to accept that infants and children get the benefit of the criterion of reciprocity: "the fundamental political relation of citizenship . . . is a relation of citizens within the basic structure of society, *a structure we enter* only *by birth* and exit only by death" (emphasis added). The dealings of adults with infants and children must satisfy the criterion of reciprocity,[37] even when doing so is "at the cost of their [the adults'] own interests in particular situations"; such dealings cannot be justified by the plea that children are not the equals of adults and that *these* children will never enter the circle of free and equal citizens because we will kill them before they do and before they realize what we have done, or will do, to them. This being so, the question arises why Rawls draws the boundary of justice, fairness and reciprocity at *birth*. This question does not seek to settle the rights of the mother over and against the unborn child. It is just the question of how it could be rational to think that the child just before birth has no rights (no status in justice, fairness, reciprocity) while the child just after birth has the rights of a citizen free and equal to other citizens. As Reiman says, a decent moral-political theory "must remain open to the possibility that as-yet-unrecognized forms of unjustified coercion may be discovered and that new rights may be needed to defend freedom against them."[38] Why should the child a week before birth be subject to the uttermost *coercion*[39] of being destroyed at someone else's "balancing of values," "ordering of values," or sheer whim?

The public reason of the United States, as manifested in the loquacious judgments of its Supreme Court, has after a quarter of a century uttered not a sentence that even appears intended to offer a rational response to that question. The response, rather, is of the form: "We are in charge; *these* are the human beings (and other entities, such as corporations) we have chosen, or now choose, to protect and *those* are not."[40] Save in its phrasing, the contempt for public *reason* is as truculent as that.[41] (This refusal has been made possible partly by the position of minority justices such as Justice Scalia, who for clearly inadequate reasons would leave to the states the fundamental question of who is and who is not entitled to the protection of the U.S. Constitution's guarantees against deprivation of life without due process of law.) The failure of public reason in action is made all the more obvious by the position of the German Constitutional Court, which has repeatedly held—albeit without following through consistently—that the constitutional right to protection of life is enjoyed by the unborn human being from the time of conception.

Rawls says that the outcome of the vote on the abortion question, "is to be seen as reasonable provided all citizens of a reasonably just constitutional regime sincerely vote in accordance with the idea of public reason."[42] The decisive votes on this question have been conducted among the fifteen or so justices involved in *Roe, Webster*, and *Casey*.[43] Do the pro-abortion votes of these citizens satisfy the requirement of being cast "sincerely . . . in accordance with the idea of public reason," in Rawls's restrictive sense of that term? I cannot think of any evidence that they were.[44] The anti-abortion arguments they faced were founded squarely on claims about the human and personal nature and status of the unborn, i.e., about the absence of any significant difference between unborn and newborn. Those claims, none of them more controversial than the rival claims about the moral rights of privacy or liberty, are not substantially addressed, even for a sentence or two, in any of the pro-abortion judgments in those cases. Addressing them would not have involved moving from public to non-public reason. A doctrine which says (as Rawls and the pro-abortion justices say) that "children must be treated as equal to adults in basic constitutional rights applicable to their situation from the day of their birth" is no less "comprehensive" and no more "public" than one that says that "children must be treated as equal to adults in basic constitutional rights applicable to their situation even before birth."

By pointing to an argument by Judith Jarvis Thomson, Rawls tries to give a "reasonable" status to pro-abortion views that are in fact unreasonable. Thomson's Rawlsian argument runs:

> First, restrictive regulation [of abortion] severely constrains women's liberty. Second, severe constraints on liberty may not be imposed in the name of considerations that the constrained are not unreasonable in rejecting. And third, the many women who reject the claim that the fetus has a right to life from the moment of conception are not unreasonable in doing so.[45]

The whole point of this argument, as Thomson makes clear, is to gain its conclusion *without contesting* the central anti-abortion claims that unborn children have a right not to be intentionally or unjustly killed and a right to the equal protection of the laws against homicide. The argument fails to meet its objective. *In the admitted absence of an argument to show that in these precise respects the unborn are a different case from (say) the newly born,* the position of the many women who reject the claim that the fetus has a right to life is indeed unreasonable. The fact that these many women, or some of them, are otherwise reasonable in no way establishes that this position of theirs is reasonable or in accordance with public reason. Just as (as Rawls says) "a comprehensive doctrine is not as such unreasonable because it leads to an unreasonable conclusion in one or even in several cases," so a person is not disentitled to the description "a reasonable person" just because she adopts an unreasonable position in one or even several cases (especially cases which so obviously engage her self-interest or other special emotional sources of bias).[46]

Having claimed that a majority decision that authorizes the free killing of the unborn "is to be seen as reasonable" and "binding on citizens by the majority principle," even if it is fallacious, erroneous, and a denial of basic justice, Rawls goes on to make several claims about anti-abortion citizens (prejudicially called by him "Catholics"):

> [1] [T]hey need not exercise the right of abortion in their own case. [2] They can recognize the right as belonging to legitimate law and therefore [3] do not resist it by force. [4] To do that would be unreasonable: it would mean attempting to impose their own, comprehensive doctrine, which a majority of other citizens who follow public reason do not accept.[47]

None of these four claims is reasonable. Claim 1 reveals the negligence that passes itself off as public reason on Rawls's side of the debate. The anti-abortion citizens are claiming, with some good arguments, that abortion is rather like slave-owning: a radical, basic injustice imposed on people deprived of the protections of citizenship. The response, "*You* free citizens need not exercise the right to [own slaves] [abort your children] in your own case, so you can and must recognize our law as legitimate as it applies to the rest of us," is mere impudence or thoughtlessness.

Claim 2 assumes that "the majority principle" is binding even when the majority authorizes gross injustice, and even when they do so without attempting to show that it is consistent with the principle or criterion of reciprocity. Does anyone believe that Rawls himself accepts this assumption in relation to injustices that engage his sympathies?

Claim 3 switches without warning into the descriptive mode. The interesting question, however, is whether there is *good reason* not to defy the law that penalizes the use of reasonable force to rescue the unborn from their killers. I can think of only one plausible reason to exclude such defiance as a conscientious option for those whose vocations are consistent with such an undertaking: that to attempt forcible rescue would generally, under present conditions, be to launch a civil war. That resultant in itself does not settle the argument. But (as I indicated above, in my remarks about the liberalism of fear) a condition for justly launching war is that one have some prospect of winning it, and that condition is not, in present circumstances, satisfied.

Claim 4 again depends on an arbitrary and unwarranted premise: that those who enforce their view that a newborn baby must be treated as equal to adults in basic rights (or who imprison pedophiles) are *not* imposing their own "comprehensive doctrine," whereas those who insist that the baby a day before birth is entitled to the same forcible protection *are*. Of course, this sort of selective inattention to the strongly substantive and controversial character of self-styled liberal theories is very characteristic of such theories; we see it in, for example, the claim that "the right of a woman's right to control her body" is "undisputed" (and therefore trumps the disputed right of the unborn child to live) when in reality the alleged right of the woman is manifestly disputed and was never accepted by any state until the Supreme Court overthrew the abortion laws of every state (and indeed it is not a right accepted even by the Supreme Court to this day). This sort of inattention often leads to outright self-contradiction, as when people say that arguments about the use of public force must never appeal to what has intrinsic value, but only to what people subjectively prefer, and then offer to justify this "principle of subjective preference" by arguing that self-governance is intrinsically valuable and/or is a necessary condition of a good—i.e., an intrinsically valuable—life![48]

Private Power versus Public Reason

The public "public reason" of the United States (and other such nations) presents, as I have said, an extraordinary spectacle: blank refusal to state any reason justifying the dramatic, radical difference in the asserted moral and posited legal status of the baby inside and the baby outside the womb, the same baby on perhaps the same day. The wider "public reason" that includes the philosophers and others who offer to guide public deliberation on the abortion question presents a different but analogous spectacle. There is an immense literature claiming to justify the right to abortion, i.e., the right to expel the fetus with intent to kill it. But this has two striking features. First, there is no consensus on the nature of the unborn child, nor on the question as to when the conceptus becomes human or a person or otherwise entitled to a right to life, nor on any other major metaphysical or moral question involved. There is no "overlapping consensus" except in the result: women are to have some opportunity to destroy their unborn children. And second, there is almost complete inattention to the substantial scholarly literature presenting the opposing position, a consensus that denies the abortion right on the basis that the conceptus has the nature and rights of a human person from conception.[49]

The silence of public "public reason" about the justification for denying to the unborn the basic equality rights acknowledged in the newly born is easy to explain. The prospects for producing such a justification are faint indeed. For any such justification will have to abandon the one real basis of human equality and equality rights, namely the fact that each living human being possesses, *actually and not merely potentially*, the *radical capacity*[50] to reason, laugh, love, repent, and choose *as this unique, personal individual*, a capacity that is not some abstract characteristic of a species but rather consists in the unique, individual, organic functioning of the organism that comes into existence as a new substance at the conception of that human being and subsists until his or her death, whether ninety minutes, ninety days, or ninety years later; a capacity, individuality, and personhood that subsists as real and precious even while its operations come and go with many changing factors such as immaturity, injury, sleep, and senility.

(It is ridiculous to say that belief in the reality and value of personhood understood in the way that I have just summarized is "religious." It is rather a belief that results from a close attention to the solidity and depth of this universe and its various constituents, the kind of close attention which is a primary *cause* of religious beliefs—and also of good science—rather than a mere result of them.)

Once one has decided not to base equality rights on the real personhood that is instantiated in the human unborn as well as the born, one will be reduced to grounding them on some factor that is not coextensive with membership of the human race and that is lacked by newborns, infants, and some mentally disabled persons. But drawing the circle around (say) sane adults and noninfant children, on the basis that they have self-awareness and concern for self, will then prove as groundless as drawing it around all and only the born. Reiman's efforts to work with self-awareness and self-concern as the basis for a right to life make this fragility manifest. (I leave to one side his half-hearted effort to show that there is some reason for "protecting infants' lives" even though no infant has—on his account—any right to life, deserves to live, or is worthy of our respect.)[51] For if my right to be respected (counted in the reciprocity criterion; not killed; etc.) depends upon my being aware of and concerned to continue my existence, why should I not be killed suddenly and without warning? Reiman says that "the loss to an aware individual of the life whose continuation she is counting on, is a loss . . . that remains a loss, a frustration of an individual's expectations . . . ."[52] But this will not do. If a sleeping individual is killed without warning, there is at no time any *individual with frustrated expectations*, and at no time any *individual suffering from a loss*. Searching around for an entity which undergoes this loss and frustration, Reiman doubles up the entities in play:

Once a human being has begun to be aware of her life, that life unfolds before a kind of inner audience that has an expectation of its continuation, an affective stake in living on. This expectation persists until the audience shuts down for good—even if, before that, the audience dozes off from time to time. We defeat this expectation even if we kill a temporarily sleeping or comatose individual who has begun to be aware of her life.[53]

But this doubling up gets Reiman nowhere. When the sleeping individual is killed without warning, the alleged audience, too, is simultaneously "shut down for good." So the plain fact remains that there is never anyone (actor or audience) of whom we can rightly say "this individual has some defeated expectations." Reiman is just equivocating on "defeated expectations," which *when someone has them* are a cause or kind of misery and often the resultant subject matter of injustice. Looking at the expectations, as Reiman invites us to do, we can see that, in the case I am considering, there never are any defeated expectations. First, there are X's *undefeated* expectations, and then, a moment later and forever after, *nothing* in the way of expectations, defeated or undefeated. There is no change *in* X's subjective awareness; that awareness simply ceases, without any awareness *of* its cessation.[54]

Reiman's entire discussion of the unborn and the early infant is, then, a timely warning that the right to life, respect, justice, and equality loses its intelligibility and its rational claim on conscientious deliberations and choices once it is uprooted from the foundations which were everywhere acknowledged as a matter of public reason until the unprincipled will to private power ("the principle of subjective preference," "choice") closed down public reason on the abortion question.

Notes

1. Jeffrey H. Reiman, *Critical Moral Liberalism: Theory and Practice*. Lanham, Md.: Rowman & Littlefield, 1997, p. 190.
2. He goes on (ibid.): "As early as a living fetus can be safely and easily removed from a pregnant woman, her right to abortion might be transformed into a duty to provide extrauterine care for her expelled fetus. If (when!) medical technology pushes this point back towards

the earliest moments of pregnancy, *the right to abortion will disappear entirely.*" (emphasis added here as elsewhere in the paper)

3. As Reiman says (ibid., p. 195), "it is so natural to us to think this way", viz. of the fetus "as a personlike victim—which is a moral status that a not-yet-existing fetus lacks." This in turn is tightly linked to the assumption, which Reiman grants and perhaps even concedes, that "the being that traverses the span from conception to death is a self-identical individual. That is more or less a natural extension of the common belief that a human being from birth to death is a self-identical individual—the one named by its proper name." (p. 194)

4. It might be called the "great misprision" of abortion, as the seventeenth and eighteenth century textbooks of English and therefore American criminal law put it. But since *Roe v. Wade*, 410 U.S. 113 (1973), a majority of states in the United States have enacted laws making killing an unborn human being at some stage of gestation a form of homicide (in some states called feticide, in some homicide, in some murder). In some states it is a homicide at whatever stage of gestation, and in a few it is murder at any stage. The validity of such laws has been upheld in the highest courts of Illinois, Minnesota, and California; the state of doctrine is reviewed and summarised in *People v. Davis* 872 P.2d 591, 599 (California Supreme Court in Banc, 1994): "[W]hen the mother's privacy interests are not at stake, the Legislature may determine whether, and at what point, it should protect life inside a mother's womb from homicide." For the state of the law, see Clark D. Forsythe, "Human Cloning and the Constitution," *Valparaiso University Law Review*, 32 (1998), 469.

5. See John Finnis, *Aquinas: Moral, Political, and Legal Theory*. Oxford and New York: Oxford University Press, 1998.

6. Aquinas argued: "[K]ings are constituted to preserve inter-personal social life {*ad socialem vitam inter homines conservandam*}; that is why they are called 'public persons,' as if to say promoters or guardians of public good. And for that reason, the laws they make direct people in their relationships with other people {*secundum quod ad alios ordinantur*}. Those things, therefore, which neither advance nor damage the common good are neither prohibited nor commanded by human laws" (Aquinas, *Opera Omnia*, vol. 14, p.

46* col. 1. See likewise *Summa Theologiae* I–II q. 96 a. 3c; q. 98 a. 1c; q. 100 a. 2c. These and other texts are considered more fully in Finnis, *Aquinas,* ch. 7.)

7. This needs qualification if and only to the extent that there are private revelations from God. So the Catholic faith claims that its own teaching is a matter of public reason, inasmuch as it is a matter of public, not private revelation; see the claim made in Peter's preaching in Jerusalem (*Acts* 2:22), in Paul's in Athens (*Acts* 17:31), and Vatican II, *Lumen Gentium* (1964) sec. 25.

8. John Rawls, *Political Liberalism.* New York: Columbia University Press, 1996, p. 220.

9. See Finnis, *Aquinas,* pp. 222–27.

10. Aquinas, *Summa Theologiae* I–II q. 94 a. 4c.

11. Ibid., I–II q. 95 a. 2c.

12. See Finnis, *Aquinas,* pp. 91 n. 141, 153 n. 91, and 246.

13. *Summa Theologiae* I–II q. 90 a. 4c.

14. Ibid., I–II q. 95 a. 3 c (laws lacking clarity in expression {*manifestatio*} are harmful).

15. Ibid., I–II q. 96 a. 1.

16. Ibid., I–II q. 97 a. 2c.

17. Ibid., I–II q. 95 a. 3c (*disciplina conveniens unicuique secundum suam possibilitatem*).

18. Aquinas thus pointed to all the main features of the Rule of Law, as Lon Fuller, *The Morality of Law,* Yale University Press 1969, p. 242, acknowledges. See Finnis, *Aquinas,* p. 257.

19. Aquinas, *Quodlibetal Questions* IV q. 9 a. 3c.

20. Similarly, Thomas Nagel, in "Moral Conflict and Political Legitimacy," *Philosophy & Public Affairs,* 16 (1987), at 229, writes: "The defense of liberalism requires that a limit somehow be drawn to appeals to the truth in political argument." For a decisive critique of both Rawls and Nagel in this regard, see Joseph Raz, *Ethics in the Public Domain.* Oxford and New York: Oxford University Press, 1994, pp. 60–96.

21. Quotations from Rawls are from *Political Liberalism,* paperback ed., pp. 137 and 217. Very often he states the principle of legitimacy expansively, so that it outlaws not only using public coercive power on certain (i.e., nonpublic) grounds, but also outlaws the

such grounds in all political discussion (at least of constitutional essentials and matters of basic justice; see pp. 214–15), even on the part of those who wish to resist that sort of use of public power (e.g., pp. 138 and 153). This expansion seems to me inevitable, for if the legitimacy principle filtered out political theses only when and because they demand the use of public power (as Rawls often suggests when setting up his legitimacy principle and trying to make it palatable), it would in many cases result only in a grotesque free-for-all of private power. Take abortion: one thesis says that public power should be used to prevent the aborting of (say) healthy children in healthy mothers. If we reject that as illegitimate just because it seeks the use of public power, we still confront the thesis of those who say that public power should be used to prevent abortion rescuers who seek to use their private power to stop the killing of fetuses just as they would try to stop the killing of infants. If we rule out this thesis because it too seeks to harness public power, we are left with a sheer power struggle between the abortionists and the rescuers. And as a matter of fact, quite appropriately, Rawls's own discussion of what theses are legitimate in relation to abortion makes no reference to the use of public power, but only to the substantive facts and political values (life, equality, nature of early as opposed to late pregnancy, and so forth, see p. 243n).

22. Rawls, *Political Liberalism*, p. 138. Note, incidentally, the tension between Rawls' approval of "uncompromising" refusal to endorse certain religious opinions, here, and his statement on p. xxvi that "political liberalism starts by taking to heart the absolute depth of [the] irreconcilable latent conflict" which is introduced when a salvationist, creedal and expansionist religion "introduces into people's conceptions of their good a transcendent element not admitting of compromise." In reality, a "transcendent element not admitting of compromise" is in no way peculiar to such religions.

23. Notice: If reasonable persons are differing about this thesis *uncompromisingly*, they must think that their own position endorsing or withholding their endorsement from it is correct. If they are modest objectivists, they will each hold that under ideal epistemic conditions—"favourable conditions of investigation" and reflection (John

Finnis, *Fundamentals of Ethics* [Washington, DC: Georgetown University Press, 1983], p. 64, citing David Wiggins, "Truth, Invention and the Meaning of Life," *Proceedings of the British Academy*, 62 [1997], 331)—reasonable people would agree with their affirmation (or denial); for (i) that is entailed by the ordinary concept of truth which modest objectivists simply unpack, and (ii) that is also the presupposition on which people engage in reasonable debate with each other (assuming that they are not mere propagandists willing to use any and every rhetorical device to win nonrational endorsements of the theses for which they are "arguing"). (So this quasi-[ideal case] prediction, unlike Rawls's apparent prediction of disagreement, is really based upon a normative, internal assessment of the rational grounds for endorsing [affirming] or denying the thesis.)

24. Consider the following passages from *Political Liberalism*: (i) "[I]n discussing constitutional essentials and matters of basic justice, we are not to appeal to comprehensive religious and philosophical doctrines—to what we as individuals or members of associations see as the whole truth . . . [but to] the plain truths now widely accepted, *or available*, to citizens generally" (pp. 224–25). (ii) "[E]ach of us must have, and be ready to explain, a criterion of what principles and guidelines we think other citizens . . . may reasonably be expected to endorse along with us . . . . Of course, we may find that actually others fail to endorse the principles and guidelines our criterion selects. That is to be expected [!]" (pp. 226–27).

25. Ibid., pp. 152–53.

26. Reiman, in his response to me, claims that I am overlooking the fact that "Rawls's notion of the burdens of judgment is an empirical claim." Not so. That phrase, as used by Rawls, is infected with precisely the same ambiguity (between normative and empirical) that infects his phrases "public reason" and "political conception." Nor does it restrain Rawls for a moment from passing adverse judgment on those who reject his claim that abortions of convenience during the first three months of gestation are obviously acceptable. Reiman, too, freely pronounces many unburdened, but eminently controvertible, judgments in his book and in his paper in this volume. As actually deployed by Rawls and Reiman, the claim about the political implications of "the burdens of judgment" is self-refuting.

Note also Reiman's remarks (i) that "Finnis is sure" that "some very good arguments will succeed in getting themselves publicly and fully established" (p. 110, in this volume) and (ii) that "Finnis cannot understand why" philosophical disputes such as those about abortion are intractable (n. 6). These remarks exemplify, in relation to public reason and natural law, precisely that inattention to opposing arguments that I say is characteristic of the defenders of abortion. Like the main theorists of the tradition from Plato through Aristotle and Aquinas to today, I have often explained why, in the nonideal conditions of human life and character which we should expect to prevail until the end of history, *no one* should anticipate, let alone "be sure," that good arguments *will* succeed in getting themselves generally—let alone fully—accepted.

27. Rawls, *Political Liberalism*, pp. 62 and 225.

28. See e.g., Finnis, *Natural Law and Natural Rights*. Oxford University Press, 1980, pp. 108–9; and "Legal Enforcement of Duties to Oneself: Kant v. Neo-Kantians," *Columbia Law Review*, 87 (1987), at 435–36.

29. See *Political Liberalism*, p. 24 n. 27.

30. Ibid., at 96 text and n. 8.

31. See Justinian, *Institutes* I ii 12: *parum est ius nosse si personae quarum causa statuum est* ignorentur (there is little point in knowing the law if one does not know about the *persons for whose sake the law was made).*

32. Rawls, *Political Liberalism*, p. 243 n. 32.

33. Bizarrely, this right is not one of Rawls's "principles of justice," and so anyone who asserts it (as in numerous Bills of Rights, though not the antique American one) is asserting a comprehensive, not a political, doctrine!

34. See John Finnis, "Is Natural Law Theory Compatible with Limited Government?" in *Natural Law, Liberalism, and Morality*, ed. Robert P. George. Oxford: Clarendon Press, 1996, at 10–11. See also Raz, *Ethics in the Public Domain*, p. 96, referring to the "intuitively appealing idea that political principles must be accessible to people as they are"—i.e., with their oversights and prejudices—and concluding that the failure of Rawls's and Nagel's arguments "suggests that the underlying idea may be at bottom unstable and incoherent."

Quotations from Rawls in this paragraph are taken from *Political Liberalism*, pp. xxiv n. 10, xxvi–xxviii, 24 n. 27, 58, and 225.

35. See also John Rawls, "The Idea of Public Reason Revisited," *University of Chicago Law Review*, 64 (1997), 765–807. Quotations in this paragraph are from *Political Liberalism*, pp. xliv–xlvi and li.

36. One can, of course, well imagine someone—inspired perhaps by Reiman's talk (in his response to me) of "enforced pregnancy" (referring not to conception by rape but to the simple requirement that women not kill their unborn babies) and by his appeal precisely in that context to the liberal position that "people are free to believe as they see fit"—saying that there must be no "forced chastity" and that in a liberal state men must be "free to believe as they see fit" that young children who are compliant (whether by virtue of drugs or other factors) should be available to sexual pro-choicers to satisfy their urgent sexual needs.

37. See also, very clearly, Rawls, A *Theory of Justice*, p. 509: "[T]he minimal requirements defining moral personality refer to a capacity and not to the realization of it. *A being that has this capacity, whether or not it is yet developed, is to receive the full protection of the principles of justice.* Since *infants and* children are thought to have basic rights (normally exercised on their behalf by parents and guardians), this interpretation . . . seems necessary to match our considered judgments. Moreover, regarding the potentiality as sufficient accords with the hypothetical nature of the original position, and with the idea that as far as possible the choice of principles should not be influenced by arbitrary contingencies. Therefore, it is reasonable to say that those who could take place in the initial agreement, were it not for fortuitous circumstances, are assured equal justice." (emphasis added) Well said.

38. Reiman, *Critical Moral Liberalism*, p. 1.

39. This must be remembered when reading Reiman's response to me, when he says "public reason is . . . *talk aimed at determining what may or may not be coerced*" and refers to the liberal's "special allergy to coercion." [Reiman, p. 110 in this volume.]

40. Reiman, in his response to me (paper in this volume, n. 7) claims that *Roe v. Wade* did not ignore or skirt the issue I am here considering: "On the contrary, the Court addressed it directly—*as a question of*

legal precedent" and "reviewed the history of the notion of legal personhood in Anglo-American law (and, in particular, as it functions in the Fourteenth Amendment to the U.S. Constitution), and concluded that 'the unborn have never been recognized in the law as persons in the whole sense.'" Reiman's claim is indefensible. There is in *Roe v. Wade* no review whatever of the "history of the notion of the legal personhood in Anglo-American law" and no mention even of Court's own holdings about the meaning of "person" in the Fourteenth Amendment. There is thus, for example, no mention of the Court's ruling in *Santa Clara County v. Southern Pacific Railroad* 118 U.S. 394 (1886), overruling precedent and holding that corporations are persons for the purposes of the Fourteenth Amendment's protection of the equal protection of the law, a ruling maintained (over reasoned dissents, never responded to) ever since. Justice Blackmun's judgment in *Roe* offers nothing of what Reiman has imagined, save a four-sentence summary of the instances in which the term "person" is used in the Constitution, followed by only two sentences: "But in *nearly* [!] all these instances, the use of the word is such that it has application only postnatally. None indicates, *with any assurance,* that it has any possible pre-natal application" (emphasis added). (The same can certainly be said of application of the Constitution's use of "person"—e.g., in connection with voting, membership of the Congress, eligibility to be president, etc. etc.—to corporations.) The "conclusion" quoted by Reiman is not a rational response to the argument of the state of Texas that the unborn have been recognized in Anglo American law—and by the constitution of Texas as interpreted by its own courts—as persons for the purposes of *relevant* legal protection, and in any event *should* now be so recognized. Nor is it a response to the question I have posed in the text. Reiman would like us to forget that the most famous American appeal to "legal precedent" to settle who is and who is not a legal person for the purposes of U.S. law is *Scott v. Sandford* 60 U.S. 393 (1857), in which the Court had little difficulty in proving from precedent, to its own satisfaction, that Negroes, even after emancipation, and even if born free, were not citizens of the United States *and could not be made citizens either by a State or by Congress.* So much for the determination of great questions of right and principle and personal status by a review restricted to precedent and uninformed by concern for persons in their prelegal reality and worth. On the grotesque inaccuracy of the references to common law, nineteenth century abortion law, and modem tort and criminal law in the Court's judgment in *Roe v. Wade,* see Robert Byrne, "An American Tragedy: The Supreme Court on Abortion," *Fordham Law Review,* 41 (1973), 807; Robert Destro, "Abortion and the Constitution: The Need for a Life-Protective Amendment," *California Law Review,* 63 (1975), 1250; James Witherspoon, "Re-examining *Roe:* Nineteenth-century Statutes and the Fourteenth Amendment," *St. Mary's Law Review,* 17 (1985), 29; David Kader, "The Law of Tortious Prenatal Death Since *Roe v. Wade,"* *Missouri Law Review,* 45 (1980), 639; Clarke D. Forsythe, "Human Cloning and the Constitution," *Valparaiso University Law Review,* 32 (1998), 469; John Finnis, "'Shameless Acts' in Colorado: Abuse of Scholarship in Constitutional Cases," *Academic Questions* 7, no. 4 (fall 1994). On the legal precedents, then, the Court's argument in *Roe* is shamefully weak; on the level of *reasons* for discriminating between the born and the unborn it has, as I state in the text above, precisely nothing to say.

41. The open unreasonableness is encapsulated in the statement by the Court in *Roe v. Wade* that "We need not resolve the difficult question of when life begins," followed by statements and rulings which presuppose and indeed assert that before birth the child's life is merely "the potentiality of human life." The same pretence of agnosticism is maintained in *Planned Parenthood v. Casey* 505 U.S. 833, 852 (1992): "Abortion . . . is an act fraught with consequences for others: for the woman . . . for the persons who perform . . . for the spouse, family and society which must confront the knowledge that these procedures exist [!], procedures which some deem [!] nothing short of an act of violence against innocent human life; and, depending on one's beliefs, for the life or potential life that is aborted."

42. Rawls, *Political Liberalism,* p. lvi.

43. *Webster v. Reproductive Health Services* 492 U.S. 490 (1989); *Planned Parenthood v. Casey* 505 U.S. 833 (1992).

44. And I heard on the radio a set of remarks in which the speaker, said by the BBC to be Justice Powell, explained that his vote in *Roe v.*

Wade was cast on the basis of what he felt he would want for his daughter if she were pregnant. This is in line with remarks made by Powell in 1979 in an interview with Harry M. Clor, quoted in David J. Garrow, *Liberty and Sexuality: The Right to Privacy and the Making of Roe v. Wade* (New York: Macmillan, 1994), p. 576, which seem utterly indifferent to the demands of the criterion of reciprocity: "The concept of liberty was the underlying principle of the abortion case—the liberty to make certain highly personal decisions that are terribly important to people. . . . It is difficult to think of a decision that's more personal or more important to a pregnant woman than whether or not she will bear a child." Like the Court's opinion in *Casey*, which on the point in issue says the same thing but in many more words, this is simply a diaphanously veiled appeal to power regardless of questions of justice. It's difficult to think of a decision that is less personal, and more important to another person, than the decision to kill that person.

45. Judith Jarvis Thomson, "Abortion," *Boston Review*, 20; 3 (1995), 15. Cf. Rawls, *Political Liberalism*, p. lvi n. 31.

46. Rawls, *Political Liberalism*, p. 244 n. 32. The fact that the three-step Thomson-Rawls argument is "clearly cast in the form of public reason" does not entail that it is reasonable: "whether it is itself reasonable or not . . . is another matter. As with any form of reasoning in public reason, the reasoning may be fallacious or mistaken" (Rawls, p. lvi n. 32, in relation to an argument attributed to Cardinal Bernadin). Step (3) of the Thomson argument equivocates on "are unreasonable."

47. Rawls, *Political Liberalism*, pp. lvi–lvii.

48. For this self-refutation, see Reiman's paper in this volume. I grant Reiman (n. 10) that formal self-contradiction can be avoided here by stipulating that the term "arguments that aim at justifying the use of coercion" shall be deemed to exclude "arguments about what justifies a liberal state in the first place." But even if the stipulation that these claims are at "different levels" and applicable to "different things" works to avoid formal self-contradiction, it fails to avert the self-refutation of the overall "liberal" *justification* of the state and of the limits of its coercive authority. For when "claims" are put on a level by being proposed as premises and conclusions of a justifying

argument, they are no longer mere unconnected assertions about "different things." Any justification for the liberal state is a justification for some state and will have to include a justification for the use of coercion (including at least the use of coercion to prevent some but not all private coercion), while, conversely, any argument defining the kinds of justified coercion will have to include (as liberal arguments do) a justification for the state. The *unjustifiable*, unprincipled character of the "principle of subjective preference" is revealed by each of Reiman's alternative assertions in n. 10, namely the assertions (i) that his response to me was making no claim about intrinsic value when it affirmed that "self-governance is the necessary condition of a life that . . . possesses *the special dignity and respect-worthiness that rationality bestows upon us,*" and (ii) that arguments about coercion in a liberal state *can,* after all, appeal to (one) intrinsic value, the dignity and respect-worthiness that rationality bestows upon us. Although Reiman's permission to appeal to that intrinsic value is all that is needed by opponents of aborting the children of the one species of *rational* animal, his strategy of justifying coercion remains incoherent.

49. The asymmetry is far reaching. Scholars opposing the abortion right labor through the myriad confused and diverse arguments for abortion (or abortion and infanticide) rights, and publish careful, well-documented critiques. Scholars favouring abortion (or abortion and a right to infanticide) seem for the most part to invent the positions they offer to refute, and display little or in most cases no awareness of the arguments actually advanced by defenders of the unborn.

50. In his response, Reiman quotes this sentence, and then, in making the assertion that my proposition "is simply false" (Reiman, p. 115 in this volume) repeats the statement but *omits the key word* "radical." For the idea of *radical capacity* (with its reference to *radix,* root), see my essays "A Philosophical Case Against Euthanasia," "The Fragile Case for Euthanasia," and "Misunderstanding the Case Against Euthanasia," in *Euthanasia Examined: Ethical, Clinical and Legal Perspectives* ed. John Keown (Cambridge, UK: Cambridge University Press, 1995), especially at pp. 31–33, 47–50, and 68–70. One can easily begin to understand the notion by reflecting on the

coherence of the statement "I have the capacity to speak Icelandic though I cannot speak it at all." Here the reference to "capacity" is to a capacity more basic (radical) than the developed capacity (nonexistent in my case) to speak the language here and now. A human zygote which has the necessary genetic primordia for development already has the capacity—radical capacity—not only to develop legs but also to use them for walking. A salmon zygote does not have this radical capacity to walk. In short, a capacity to develop, by autonomous natural growth, a capacity to X is an already actual radical capacity to X. It is not "distant from" capacity X, let alone "too distant"; it is precisely capacity X in its earliest form.

51. Reiman, *Critical Moral Liberalism*, 202–03, offers to explain why "we" think it is wrong to kill infants, but has nothing to say which could show the immorality of the attitudes of someone who does not "love infants" (but only perhaps two or three infants) and thinks it is not wrong to kill infants (at least infants not loved in particular by anybody particular).

52. Reiman, *Critical Moral Liberalism*, p. 197.

53. Reiman, *Critical Moral Liberalism*, p. 198.

54. In his response, Reiman misses the point comprehensively. He imagines that while he is debating with me, the house he intends to return to burns down. He says he has frustrated expectations even if he doesn't know that the house has burned down, and that fact about the frustration of his expectations is not negated by his subsequent death on the way home. I of course agree that *if* his expectations were frustrated by the burning of the house unbeknownst to him—which I grant for the sake of argument but do not concede—that fact would not be negated by his subsequent death. But my argument, from beginning to end, is that the event of causing instantaneous death, without warning, cannot be said to frustrate expectations; there is in such a case no other event that could be said to frustrate them and no time span, such as Reiman assumes in which expectations might be said to be, or have been, frustrated. Remember, this whole debate about expectations arises only because Reiman wants to make *awareness of one's life* the trait which accounts for one's having rights. "Frustration," which one is forever unaware of should, I argue, count for nothing in such a perspective.

But the concept and reality of *harm* is not restricted to that perspective, which is why, as Reiman observes, being killed, even without—or, I add, before—one's awareness, is a grievous form of harm and violation of rights.

Jeffrey Reiman

Abortion, Natural Law, and Liberal Discourse: A Response to John Finnis

I AGREE WITH PROFESSOR FINNIS that the legality of abortion must be publicly determined. It cannot be left as a private choice on the grounds that it is not amenable to resolution within the limits of what John Rawls has characterized as "public reason." In fact, I shall argue that it is amenable to such resolution. While I do not endorse Rawls's notion of public reason in all its details, I think that the idea contains an important piece of political wisdom that Professor Finnis is missing. I shall try to sketch out a conception of public reason that makes this wisdom more evident. Along the way, I shall point out what the place of natural law arguments of the sort proposed by Professor Finnis is with respect to the terms of public reason. I shall then suggest how abortion is in fact amenable to resolution within these terms and, in passing, I shall respond to some of Professor Finnis's objections to my views about abortion.[1]

In his important book *Political Liberalism*, John Rawls argues that there are limits on the kinds of reasons that can be used to justify laws and policies in a liberal state. Rawls presents a design for a politically liberal society in which people with differing moral and theological views can form a moral consensus about the guiding values of their shared political existence. Hence his conception of public discourse is governed by the idea of reciprocity, according to which arguments about public legal measures are to be made in terms that each believes the others, though differing in their moral and theological views, can accept. Rawls has called political discourse that is subject to these limits "public reason."[2] The idea is that "citizens are to conduct their public political discussions of constitutional essentials and matters of basic justice within the framework of what each sincerely regards as a reasonable political conception of justice, a conception that expresses political values that others as free and equal also might reasonably be expected reasonably to endorse."[3]

Rawls characterizes his liberalism as "political" to distinguish it from liberalism that is based on a comprehensive moral or metaphysical or religious doctrine and that, as a result, puts itself forth as true for all, regardless of their personal moral and theological views. My own conception of liberalism is what Rawls would call a comprehensive doctrine. It is based on a theory of the nature of the good life, though the theory claims to spell out no more than a necessary condition of the good life. The necessary condition is that one live a life that is in large measure a product of one's own choices and judgments—what I shall call generally a "self-governed life." Since lives can be governed well or poorly, the fact that a life is self-governed does not guarantee that it will be good. However, it being self-governed is a necessary condition of it being good for three reasons, which I will state very briefly here:[4]

1. Self-governance is a necessary condition of a life that one can call one's own accomplishment, and as such it is a necessary condition of a life that has a special kind of significance for the one whose life it is.
2. Self-governance is a necessary condition of a life that answers to the fact of our mortality. Following Heidegger (with some license), I think that mortality confronts us with the imperative to live a life

that coincides with our own sense of what makes a life worth living, and thus a life that must be the outcome of our own judgments about what makes a life worth living.

3. Self-governance is the necessary condition of a life that expresses one's nature as a rational being, and thus a life that possesses the special dignity and respect-worthiness that rationality bestows upon us.

The upshot of these considerations, in my view, is that it is a necessary condition of people living good lives that they be allowed freely to formulate and enact their own judgments about how best to live, as far, of course, as this is compatible with allowing all people the same freedom. For this reason, plus the fact that preserving freedom allows people of all different beliefs to live together peacefully, I contend that there is a moral obligation to comply with the principles of liberalism that is based on reasons that override individuals' personal moral and theological views. This is what makes my view a comprehensive doctrine in Rawls's terms. Consequently, while I agree with Rawls that there are appropriate limits on the terms of liberal political discourse, I think that they need to be stated more specifically than he does, and that they must be shown more clearly to relate to the core ideal of liberalism understood as a comprehensive moral doctrine.

A liberal state is one that accepts the imperative of protecting the freedom of people (sane adults, that is) to formulate and enact their own judgments about how best to live, and thus in particular it is a state that accepts the idea that force is not to be used to impose the judgments of some people about what constitutes a good life on others against their will—beyond, of course, the goodness of freely chosen lives. None of this precludes, in my view, the state playing a role in informing people about what choices are available, about what experience teaches about the consequences of certain choices, and thus even advocating certain choices over others. What is ruled out is forcing people to live this way or that, beyond what is needed to protect every sane adult's chances of living as he or she sees fit.

It is this last consideration that leads to constraints on the terms of debate about the use of force. To understand these constraints and their place in a liberal state, it will help to distinguish *public reason* (which is aimed at justifying coercive laws) from *public discussion* (which is aimed at seeking voluntary agreement). Professor Finnis thinks that appeals to natural law, being eminently rational and reasonable, cannot reasonably be excluded from public political debate in a liberal state. And, to be sure, they cannot be excluded from public discussion. There is a principle of freedom of expression in a liberal state that leaves it open to all participants to say and think what they please. But public reason is something different. It is not just general talk about what's good or bad to do, *it is talk aimed at determining what may or may not be legally coerced.* It is because of the special commitment of liberal states to freedom, their special "allergy" to coercion, that the terms upon which coercion may be justified are restricted in a way that general public discussion may not be. Public reason, then, is discussion limited so as to rule out justifying laws that force people to live according to other people's judgments of how best to live.

According to Finnis, Rawls thinks that doctrines like that of natural law should be excluded from public reason because what Rawls calls "the burdens of judgment" (basically a list of reasons why intelligent people of good will will be unlikely to reach agreement on fundamental views)[5] imply that holders of such doctrines are "'mistaken' in thinking that their beliefs can be 'publicly and fully established by reason'." Finnis objects that this claim can only be made about a particular doctrine by considering its arguments. It's always possible that some very good arguments will succeed in getting themselves publicly and fully established by reason, and Finnis is sure that this is so of the arguments for natural law. What Finnis is overlooking here is that Rawls's notion of the burdens of judgment is an empirical claim, and one that is quite well supported, for example, by conferences such as the one at which Professor Finnis and I presented these papers, where intelligent people of good will arrive convinced of their own views, listen to the well-formed arguments of people with other views, and normally go home still convinced of their own views.[6]

So, Professor Finnis can rail at "public reason" in the United States for its "blank refusal to state any reason justifying the dramatic, radical, total difference in the moral and legal status of the baby inside and the baby outside the womb; the same baby on perhaps the same day."[7] And others such as myself will respond: "Blank refusal?—you've stated one of the reasons in your denial that reasons have been stated: the baby inside the womb is *inside a womb*, which is to say, inside, connected to, and living off a woman, such that treating it as if it had the same rights as a born baby entails either forcing a woman to stay pregnant against her will or invading her body to remove the fetus." Such arguments as Professor Finnis is certain will be resolved by reason often come down to differences in judgment about which is the more important moral consideration, the sameness of the baby just before and just after birth, or the need to avoid subjecting a woman to such extreme coercion; or for that matter, the ownership by the woman of her body. It is precisely the empirical (not logical or philosophical) intractability of such differences in judgment, the fact that people can make these different judgments and still count as intelligent people of good will, that Rawls means by the "burdens of judgment." And for Rawls, this is a good reason for excluding from public reason doctrines that are likely to lead to intractable differences—though not of course excluding them from public discussion.

It may be objected that parity of reason implies that if this is reason to exclude natural law doctrine from public reason, then it is equally reason to exclude from public reason the doctrine that forced pregnancy is bad or a violation of a woman's ownership of herself—and then we are at a stalemate, in which the defenders of the unborn and the defenders of the pregnant have equal claims. I think that there are two liberal answers to this, one simple, the other more complex. The simple answer is that a liberal society is not neutral about coercion, and thus, since the moral status of the pregnant woman is not in doubt, a liberal society must view forced pregnancy as at least presumptively a very grave evil. Since, by contrast, the moral status of the fetus is controversial, it cannot outweigh the uncontroversially presumed evil of forcing a woman to stay pregnant against her will. It is something like this, I think, that makes "pro-choice" an appropriate liberal political position. A pro-choicer needn't think it a settled or self-evident moral fact that ending a fetus's life is so morally inconsequential as to be obviously trumped by the pregnant woman's right to control her body. Rather, a pro-choicer may think that the fact that the moral status of the fetus's life is disputed means that a position on its moral status ought not to override the undisputed right of a woman to control her body,[8] at least not in a liberal state where people are free to believe as they see fit, and can be expected to disagree about numerous important moral issues.[9]

The more complex answer lies in saying a bit more about the terms of public reason, and what kind of argument can be made within those terms about the status of the fetus. Because a liberal society promotes and protects the possibility of people living lives based on their own choices and judgments, and because this is a necessary condition of the good life for all, all are morally obligated to comply with its terms, in particular the terms in which it allows force to be justified, given the centrality of freedom. And these terms specify a special mode of political discourse, which is more or less akin to what Rawls calls public reason, but which I shall formulate with a different emphasis and call "liberal discourse." The shape of this discourse is given by two general principles, which I shall call the *principle of subjective preference*, and the *principle of individual priority*. Note that these principles apply only to public discussions that aim at justifying the use of coercion. In all other areas, at least among adults, a liberal society tolerates no substantive limits on the terms of discourse.

The principle of subjective preference holds that arguments should be made in terms of what people want to have or avoid (under which I include what they choose for or against and what they value or disvalue, plus whatever is needed for people to identify their true wants), rather than in terms of what has intrinsic value. The principle doesn't deny that some things have value in themselves, it only rules out appeal to such value for the purpose of arguments about the use of public force.[10] One shouldn't overestimate how much will be ruled out by such arguments, since most things that are plausible candidates for intrinsic value are either also wanted or valued by people (say, great paintings or beautiful natural settings), or they are part of background conditions (such as education or free expression) that enable people to identify what they truly want or value. The reason for the principle of subjective preference is that appeal to intrinsic value that does not correspond to what people themselves value or desire risks imposing judgments on people, whereas liberalism is committed to protecting their ability to make their lives the outcome of their own judgments.[11]

The principle of individual priority holds that what a person wants or desires for herself has a very strong presumption over what any number of others want or desire for her. Here, too, it should be obvious how this principle supports the liberal attempt to promote freedom and limit the use of force.

The principles of subjective value and individual priority yield the distinction between primary and secondary value. *Primary value* is that which is bestowed upon something desired by an individual for him or herself, and *secondary value* is that bestowed upon something desired by someone for someone else. Because of the primacy it gives to individual freedom, a liberal society is committed to almost never allowing secondary value—no matter how many people desire it—to trump primary value. I say *almost* never, since there may be situations where a very widely and strongly desired secondary value might prevail over a narrowly and weakly desired primary value. For example, the desire of some to walk around in the nude or to display obscene pictures or signs might be limited in light of the desire of others not to have to see such things. The liberal solution to such problems normally takes the form of some sort of zoning compromise, in which a limited area (nudist colonies, red-light zones) is set aside to permit the unpopular activity to exist for those who desire it, while leaving the others able not to have to see it. Needless to say, this won't apply to abortion since the desire for it is a strong one and, for better or for worse, widely experienced (by about a 1.5 million American women a year).

What I wish to do in the remainder of this essay is suggest how the abortion problem can be resolved subject to the constraints of liberal discourse, that is, the principles of subjective preference and individual priority. We get a little jump on the abortion question by reflecting on the odd nature of the right to life that pro-lifers think fetuses have and that pro-choicers generally deny that fetuses have. It is the same right to life that adults and children have, and it is strange because it treats life as having *asymmetric value*. That is, normally, when we take some X to have some value, we take that value to be a reason for not destroying existing Xs and a reason for creating new Xs. And, with certain minor modifications having to do with the uncertainty of the future and the difference between effort already undertaken and effort newly invested (which considerations are too small to bear on the abortion issue), we take the value of some X to be roughly *equally* a reason for not destroying existing Xs and for creating new Xs. In short, value is normally temporally *symmetric;* it casts its glow backwards and forwards in time with just about the same intensity.

One implication of temporally symmetric value is that destroying a valuable X and not creating one are (again with only minor differences) equally bad. And this is enough to show that the value that we place on the lives of those we think have a right to life is not temporally symmetric, since if it were, murder and refusal to produce new living human beings would be just about equally bad, which they are not. Users of contraceptives and fertile couples who choose to remain childless may be selfish, but they are nowhere near to being murderers. Consequently, to hold that a fetus has the same right to life as a human child or adult is to hold that it would be much worse to kill a fetus than to not produce one, and that implies that one believes that the fetus's life has asymmetric value.

It follows that if there is to be some rational ground for attributing a right to life to humans at any stage (fetus or child or adult), then the human at that stage must have some trait that accounts for its asymmetrical value. And this is a surprisingly, and usefully, restrictive condition! It immediately rules out any attribution of the right to life to humans based on whatever is good about humans: their rationality, or capacity for creativity or attachment or the like. Such good things bestow value roughly equally on future humans as on existing ones, and thus cannot account for how much worse we think it is to end an existing life than not to create a new one. It should be obvious that that applies to what Finnis—in arguing for the wrongness of abortion from conception on—asserts is "the one real basis of human . . . rights, namely the fact that each living human being possesses, *actually and not merely potentially*, the *radical capacity* to reason, laugh, love, repent, and choose *as this unique, personal individual*, a capacity which . . . comes into existence . . . at the conception of that human being and subsists until his or her death. . . ."

Actually, there are two problems with this claim, both fatal: First of all, the notion that a newly conceived zygote or even a fairly developed fetus possesses, actually and not merely potentially, the capacity to reason, laugh, love, repent and choose, is simply false. Finnis's mistake here is to confuse the capacity (which the zygote or fetus surely has) to develop a brain that has the capacity to reason and the rest, with the capacity itself (which the zygote or fetus surely lacks). This is equivalent to confusing the capacity to develop legs with the capacity to walk.[12] Second, but most important for our purposes here, the goodness of beings with such capacities is as much a reason for creating new ones as for not destroying existing ones, and thus cannot account for how much worse we think it is to end an existing life than not to create a new one.

Here, intriguingly, the asymmetry in our valuation of human life converges with the principles of liberal discourse; or, as I would prefer to believe, here our valuation of human life shows its deep liberal roots. When we ask what it is about human life that could account for asymmetric value, the only plausible answer is that at some point humans are aware of their own particular existence and care strongly about, or at least count strongly upon, continuing to stay alive.[13] Respecting this caring or counting leads to valuing already existing humans once they have begun to care about and count on staying alive. The caring about and counting on living that I have in mind here gives us reason to protect existing beings who so care and count. It does not cast a moral glow forward calling upon us to create new ones who will care about staying alive, because nothing is said about the intrinsic goodness of beings like that existing (though of course neither is anything denied about such intrinsic goodness). Thus it accounts for the asymmetrical way in which we value human life within the constraints of the liberal principle of subjective preference.[14]

Note that I am not saying that killing a child or an adult is wrong because it frustrates an occurrent desire to stay alive. My point rather is that once such caring awareness of one's life comes on the scene, an expectation of staying alive emerges, which is, so to speak, a property of the being in whom it emerges, from that point on. Killing such a being, even in its sleep, frustrates that expectation and, I contend, the wrongness of this grounds the asymmetrical right to life. Now, Professor Finnis seems to think that an expectation can only be frustrated for someone who is conscious of the frustration, and thus he thinks that my view does allow for killing people in their sleep, and so on. I think he's just wrong about this. If, as I sit here, my house is burning to the ground unbeknownst to me, at this very moment my expectation of having a house to return to is being frustrated. And that will stay true of me even if I'm killed on my way home tonight and thus never find out about the frustration.[15]

Fetuses do not yet possess the trait—the subjective awareness that they have a life and (thus) the caring about that life—that would account for their having asymmetrical value and thus a right to life. Thus, argumentation within the limits of liberal discourse leads to a defense of the pro-choice position, since the pregnant woman clearly does have such awareness of and caring about her life, not to mention autonomy rights over her body.[16]

It will trouble some people that the same argument implies that newborn infants, at least for a while, also lack the trait that would account for their having a right to life. But this does not mean that there is no liberal objection to infanticide. What it means is that the liberal objection to infanticide is based on considerations different from the liberal objection to murder. These considerations have to do with what I called above secondary value—the desires that human beings have for beings other than themselves. The fact is that human beings have deep and natural (usually, though not exclusively) positive feelings towards infants. Since I think this positive feeling is widespread, natural, and deeply felt it bestows value, albeit of a secondary sort, on the lives of infants.[17] And since such value can be promoted without running afoul of what those infants' mothers want for themselves, we have a strong secondary value that conflicts with no primary value and thus may rightly prevail. Thus we get a liberal basis for the protection of infants' lives.

That this latter protection is weaker than that accorded to beings who care about their own lives, and weaker than a woman's right to control her body, conforms to the principle of individual priority. A child's or adult's right to protection of her life, as well as a woman's right to control her body, are primary values since they are rooted in the concerned individual's preferences for herself. The rights of infants are secondary values, since they are rooted in the preferences of others.[18]

This need not be thought of as yielding the final, comprehensive truth about the morality of abortion (though I am inclined to believe that it does). What it yields, at least, is a political truth about what can rightly be legally coerced in a liberal state. Any other position must seek to obtain voluntary conviction and compliance, and that is the role that liberalism leaves to natural law doctrine and its kin. To be sure, if Rawls thinks that all citizens of a liberal state, including those with deep religious objections to abortion, will find this argument (or the one that Rawls suggests in an already infamous footnote to *Political Liberalism*)[19] *reasonable* according to their comprehensive doctrines, I think he's mistaken. Rather, liberalism enables us to say to such people and others, "Whether or not you think this is reasonable according to your comprehensive doctrines, the goodness of the life protected for you by liberalism obligates you to comply with its outcome."

Notes

1. This essay is a revised version of a paper delivered at the American Political Science Association Panel on "Natural Law, Liberalism, and Public Reason," Washington, D.C. (August 30, 1997). I thank Chris Wolfe, Stephen Macedo, John Finnis, and members of the audience for their helpful and challenging comments. I have developed and presented the views on abortion that are summarized here in Jeffrey Reiman, "Abortion, Infanticide, and the Asymmetric Value of Life," *Journal of Social Philosophy*, 27, no. 3 (winter 1996), 181–200; "Abortion, Infanticide, and the Changing Grounds of the Wrongness of Killing: Reply to Don Marquis's 'Reiman on Abortion,' *Journal of Social Philosophy*, 29, no. 2 (fall 1998); and *Abortion and the Ways We Value Human Life*. Lanham, Md.: Rowman and Littlefield, 1999. In the latter book I reply at greater length to the arguments of Finnis and others against the moral permissibility of abortion, and I show how both my argument and that of Justice Blackmun in *Roe v. Wade* (410 U.S. 113 [1973]) fit the terms appropriate to public discourse in a liberal society.

2. John Rawls, *Political Liberalism*. New York: Columbia University Press, 1993, pp. 212–54. Rawls has clarified and modified his conception of public reason in the introduction to the paperback edition of

Political Liberalism. New York: Columbia University Press, 1996, pp. l–lvii.

3. Rawls, *Political Liberalism*, p. 1 (this and all references below are from the paperback edition).

4. I develop at length a theory of the liberal conception of the good life in Jeffrey Reiman, *Critical Moral Liberalism*. Lanham, Md: Rowman & Littlefield, 1997, esp. pp. 16–18.

5. See Rawls, *Political Liberalism*, pp. 54–58.

6. For those who were not in attendance (see n. 1), I offer in evidence the following, from Finnis's paper in this volume, note 49: "Scholars opposing the abortion right labor through the myriad confused and diverse arguments for abortion (or abortion and infanticide) rights, and publish careful, well-documented critiques. Scholars favoring abortion (or abortion and infanticide) seem for the most part to invent the positions they offer to refute, and display little or in most cases no awareness of the arguments actually advanced by defenders of the unborn." If a scholar of the stature and ability of Professor Finnis can have such an extremely one-sided view of the philosophical dispute about abortion, is it any wonder that such disputes can be, in fact, intractable, and that Finnis cannot understand why?

7. Insofar as Professor Finnis's assertion here is directed at the Supreme Court's decision in *Roe v. Wade*, it is quite misleading in suggesting that the Court irresponsibly ignored or skirted this issue. On the contrary, the Court addressed it directly, *as a question of legal precedent*. Justice Blackmun, writing for the majority, reviewed the history of the notion of legal personhood in Anglo-American law (and, in particular, as it functions in the Fourteenth Amendment to the U.S. Constitution), and concluded that "the unborn have never been recognized in the law as persons in the whole sense" (*Roe v. Wade* 410 U.S. 113, 162 [1973]).

Finnis states (n. 40) that my claim here is "indefensible. There is in *Roe v. Wade* no review whatever of the 'history of the notion of legal personhood in Anglo American law' and no mention even of the Court's own holdings about the meaning of 'person' in the Fourteenth Amendment." Finnis contends that there is only a 'four-sentence summary' of the instances of the term "person" in the Constitution, and a two-sentence conclusion. That Finnis does not agree with the Court's review of the legal meaning of "person" is no surprise. His claim that it does not exist, or that it is limited to some six sentences, is, however, very hard to comprehend. Blackmun's discussion of this issue runs from page 156 to page 162 of the decision, though about two pages of this is devoted to the history of moral and religious beliefs about when life begins and thus is, though relevant to the issue, not strictly legal analysis. The rest—four pages of text plus several footnotes—is devoted to legal analysis comprised of the instances of "person" in the Constitution; mention of ten decisions "where the issue was squarely presented" that are held to be in accord with the majority's view; legal confirmation drawn from "areas other than criminal abortion," including the "traditional rule of tort law;" discussion of a number of recent developments, some of which tend away from the majority's view; and two footnotes on how the Texas statute itself is not compatible with the idea that the fetus is a legal person. I leave it to the reader to look at *Roe v. Wade* and decide for him or herself whether it supports Finnis's assertion that the "Supreme Court has, after a quarter of a century, uttered not a sentence that even appears intended to offer a rational response to that question," namely, why the fetus before birth lacks the rights that the infant has upon birth.

8. Finnis calls it "selective inattention . . . characteristic of [liberal] theories" when I assert that the woman's right to control her body is undisputed, because, he writes, this right was "manifestly disputed . . . until the Supreme Court overthrew the abortion laws of every state." Apparently, Finnis has taken me to be saying that the woman's right to an abortion is or was undisputed, which, of course, is not so, nor do I say it is so. More careful attention to my words will confirm that what I was talking about was the implication, for the legality of abortion, of the conflict between the right that women undisputedly had to control their bodies *before that right was thought to include abortion* and the disputed moral status of the fetus.

9. See, for example, Ronald Dworkin, *Life's Dominion*. New York: Vintage Books, 1994, esp. ch. 6, where Dworkin contends that the competing views about the value of the lives of fetuses are effectively religious (or sufficiently religious-like) conceptions, and as such are

barred from enforcement by the Constitution's guarantee of free exercise of religion.

10. Finnis holds (n. 48, and accompanying text) that I refute myself when I say "that arguments about the use of force must never appeal to what has intrinsic value . . . and then justify this . . . by arguing that self-governance . . . is a necessary condition of a good—i.e., an intrinsically valuable—life!" First of all, all the reasons that I gave early in this paper for why self-governance is a necessary condition of a good life could be expressed in terms of what people commonly want in and of their lives, namely, significance, felt worth in the face of death, and respect—without claiming that self-governed lives are intrinsically valuable. However, even if my view were that a self-governed life were intrinsically valuable, there would be no contradiction whatsoever in holding that, in light of this intrinsic value, arguments about coercion should not appeal to what has intrinsic value because doing so threatens people's ability to live self-governed lives. There's no contradiction here because the claim about the intrinsic value of self-governed lives is about what justifies a liberal state in the first place, while the claim about what can be appealed to in arguments for coercion is about how a liberal state should be governed. Since the claims operate at different levels of the argument and apply to different things, they do not come into conflict with one another and so they cannot contradict each other. Indeed, the argument would avoid self-contradiction if it simply said that in a liberal state, only one intrinsic value, that of self-governed lives, can be appealed to in arguments about coercion. Any way you take it, there's no self-refutation here at all.

11. For theoretical reasons, discussion of which would take us beyond the limits of this paper, liberals treat the legislative enactment of taxes, though backed up by public coercion, as a matter less threatening to freedom than laws directly concerning conduct. Thus, as long as the legislative process is fair and representative ("no taxation without representation"), and as long as certain crucial areas are protected from encroachment, say, by a "bill of rights," liberals will generally allow that people may be forced to pay taxes for projects voted by the majority. This is one area in which liberals distinguish themselves from libertarians.

12. Finnis thinks (n. 50) that calling this capacity *radical* will protect his claim from my objection here; but whatever you call it, it is not the capacity to reason, laugh and the rest, as normally understood, but something else. And that something else is too distant from what is normally understood to be a real capacity to reason or laugh to support the claim that beings with this *radical* capacity are "real and precious" persons.

13. It might seem that we could value existing fetuses asymmetrically because each is a distinct particular with its own genetic code. Thus, this line of thought runs, we could value the particular fetus itself and regard its ending as a loss of a particular that cannot be made good by replacing it with a new one, since the new fetus would be a different one with a different genetic code. This implies, to be sure, that it is logically possible to value asymmetrically the particular fetus that a pregnant woman is carrying. However, there is no reasonable ground for valuing that particular fetus asymmetrically. This is because, until the fetus develops recognizable distinctive traits, its particularity is purely negative. We simply know that it has a distinct genetic code that is different from other ones. We do not know the positive content of this difference. Without that positive content, there is no reason to prefer this particular one over a new one, which would be particular in just the same way. Thus, while the fetus's possession of a unique genetic code is a *possible* ground of asymmetric value, it is not a *plausible* ground.

14. It need not be thought that this is the only way in which human life obtains asymmetrical value, though I contend that other ways will also presuppose the individual's awareness of his ongoing life. So, for example, once humans reach a level of rationality at which they are aware of their life as, so to speak, the arena of their own happening—the stage upon which they will live the lives they want to live or fail at that—they come increasingly to earn entitlement to autonomy rights, in terms of which we no longer simply protect their lives, but additionally their ability to make of their lives what they will. Needless to say, such rights will also protect them against being killed and replaced, and thus treat them as having asymmetric value. This also implies that people who become, say, suicidal still have a

right to life due to their autonomy rights, even if strictly speaking they no longer care about continuing.

15. Finnis contends (n. 52, and accompanying text) that, since death snuffs out the life of the one who expects to go on, and since before death that individual's expectations were not yet frustrated, "there is never anyone . . . of whom we can rightly say 'this individual has some defeated expectations.'" That Finnis is off base here is clear as soon as it is recognized that his argument would also entail that no individual is harmed by being killed in his sleep. Since the victim was not harmed before being killed and is no longer there afterwards, there will never be anyone of whom we can rightly say "this individual is harmed." In any event, even if Finnis's argument were sound, we could still say, of the individual killed while he sleeps, that there *was* an individual whose expectations got frustrated (and who was thereby harmed); and, prospectively, of a living individual, we can say that he *is* an individual whose expectations would be frustrated by his being killed (and who would thereby be harmed). Either is enough for my purposes.

Finnis writes further (in his n. 52) that since I want "to make *awareness of one's life* the trait which accounts for having rights, ['f]rustration' which one is forever unaware of should . . . count for nothing in such a perspective." The trait I actually appeal to (see text accompanying my n. 13) is beings' awareness "of their own particular existence *and car[ing] strongly about, or at least count[ing] strongly upon, continuing to stay alive*" (emphasis added). It is quite widely accepted that frustration of such caring counts morally even if the subject is forever unaware of the frustration. One example of this would be the wrongness of frustrating the wishes a person expressed in his will.

16. See note 8, above.

17. Finnis takes me (n. 51) to be saying that only people who love infants have a reason not to kill them, but my claim is that because of the natural and widespread love of infants, everyone has a powerful reason—respect for what their fellows care deeply about—for not killing infants, in light of the fact that infants' lives can be protected without forcing women to stay pregnant against their will.

18. Similar things could be said about the severely retarded or senile, if (which I think is only very rarely the case) they are thought to lack

awareness of and caring about their ongoing lives. They are still the object of general human affection and have secondary value in the same way that infants do.

19. Rawls, *Political Liberalism*, p. 243 n. 32.

Paul J. Weithman

Citizenship and Public Reason

Introduction

John Rawls opens his latest treatment of public reason by saying that "[t]he idea of public reason, as I understand it, belongs to a conception of a well ordered constitutional democratic society".[1] That the idea belongs to the conception of a *well ordered* society raises obvious questions about its bearing on societies that are not well ordered, as I assume the contemporary United States is not.[2] For it could be that Rawls intends his discussion of public reason to do no more than furnish details about the conduct of political debate in a well-ordered society, details that previous descriptions left unstated. While the details would then round out Rawls's theory of justice, it would have no more (or less) bearing on actual societies than, say, his discussion of justice between generations.

If this were the right way to understand Rawls's treatment of public reason, then many criticisms of that discussion would misfire rather badly, since they presuppose that the requirements of public reason apply to us. There are, however, reasons for thinking that this is not the correct interpretation of Rawls's discussion and that his guidelines of public reason are intended to apply to actual societies and their citizens. One is his treatment of issues like abortion.[3] Both the tone in which he discusses these issues and the examples of arguments bearing on them which he takes up suggest that he thinks citizens in actual societies are required to abide by the guidelines of public reason when they debate these matters. Even more telling is the fact that Rawls's original discussion of public reason made provision for societies that are not well ordered.[4] When he later decided to drop these provisions, he commented that his revised account "secures what is needed."[5] The implication is that this revised account is intended to cover everything covered by the original one, including cases in which society is not well ordered. If it is intended to apply to liberal democracies that are not well ordered, then it is presumably intended to apply to ours. Perhaps Rawls's opening remark should therefore be understood to say that "the idea of public reason belongs to a conception of a well-ordered constitutional democratic society" in this sense: no society is well ordered unless its citizens and public officials comply perfectly with the requirements of public reason. This does not imply that the guidelines of public reason express requirements binding *only* in well-ordered societies or that they *do not* bind in actual ones.

I am especially interested in how those requirements apply to ordinary citizens in actual societies—citizens who are not public officials, running for office, or visibly associated with political campaigns. But pursuing this interest might be thought misguided. For it might seem that the requirements of public reason as Rawls conceives them apply primarily to citizens who are in these positions, and only derivatively to those who are not. While Rawls has insisted from the outset that they apply only to argument in the public forum, his most recent writing makes explicit, in a way that the earlier ones did not, just how narrow a range of political argument that encompasses. Rawls now says that "the public political forum" consists of "the discourse of judges in their decisions . . . the discourse of government officials, especially chief executives and legislators; and finally, the discourse of candidates for public office and their campaign managers, especially in their public oratory, party platforms, and political statements."[6] Ordinary citizens, Rawls continues, "fulfill their duty of civility and support the idea of public reason by doing what they can to hold government officials to it."[7]

These new qualifications notwithstanding, the requirements public reason imposes on the discourse of ordinary citizens and on the grounds of their votes remain of interest.

For one thing, Rawls explicitly says that citizens must cast votes the basis of which they are prepared to explain using public reasons.[8] Even if ordinary citizens do not put forward arguments in the public political forum, the constraints of public reason apply to them. For another, if it is widely believed that citizens will vote only for candidates who honor the requirements those guidelines express, this provides a strong incentive for candidates to honor them. The belief that citizens will vote in this way could become widespread only if citizens were prepared to explain the grounds of their votes to one another. The discourse in which they would do so could itself be subject to requirements of public reason.[9]

For still another, if American politics were reformed along lines advocated by deliberative democrats, then ordinary citizens would engage in considerably more public deliberation than they do now.[10] That deliberation would take place in public fora of some kind and at least some of it would concern constitutional essentials and matters of basic justice. Reforms that make American politics more deliberative would thereby make it possible for citizens who are not public officials to engage in the sort of discourse to which the guidelines of public reason apply. Since Rawls now says that a well-ordered democracy would be a deliberative one[11] and since he thinks American society should be well ordered, I assume he would endorse such reforms. It is important to attend to the requirements he thinks would bind ordinary citizens if the reforms he presumably endorses were enacted.

Finally, the discourse to which public reason applies must have certain special features that distinguish it from political speech in what Rawls calls "the background culture"[12] and that account for the fact that public reason applies to it. Rawls says little about what those features are.[13] Clearly he thinks more forms of political speech exhibit those features than the ones he singles out as taking place in "the public political forum," since the arguments offered by Martin Luther King, Jr. and Joseph Bernardin do not fall into any of the three categories that Rawls says constitute that forum. Yet they are said to be cast in the form of public reason.[14] This might be taken to imply that discourse in "the public political forum" is just one part of the discourse to which the idea of public reason applies. Or it might be thought to imply that a great deal more takes place in "the public political forum" than Rawls mentions. I incline to the second, thinking that some clerical speech takes place in the public forum even though Rawls does not explicitly say so.[15] It is impossible to prove that one of these conclusions is right and the other wrong, since the denotation of the phrase "public forum" is underdetermined by intuition and must ultimately be fixed by stipulation. What matters for present purposes is this: If discourse by citizens who are not public officials can exhibit those features of discourse in the public forum in virtue of which public reason applies to it, then public reason applies to discourse by ordinary citizens as well. The guidelines it imposes on them are worthy of attention.

Though Rawls is not entirely clear about it, I believe that his requirements of public reason are best understood as role-specific duties of citizenship rather than as prima facie moral obligations of persons who happen to live in a democracy. The claim that those requirements apply to citizens like us in societies like ours therefore depends upon a further claim about the validity of the conception of citizenship with which they are associated. The requirements of public reason can be our role-specific duties, binding on us, only if that conception of citizenship is an appropriate conception for us. The questions of whether it is, and of where exactly it goes wrong if it is not, are among the most interesting to ask of Rawls's discussion. Pursuing them shows that that account touches on some of the deepest issues in political philosophy.

Debates about public reason are sometimes thought to lack philosophical import or to derive their interest solely from the resurgence of the religious right in American politics. In fact what is at stake is nothing less than the nature of democratic citizenship. I shall suggest that Rawls's conception of citizenship is *not* the most appropriate one for determining the role-specific duties of ordinary American citizens and that the requirements of public reason are *not* among those duties. Ordinary citizens may put forward a much wider array of arguments than Rawls's account of public reason permits. They may not, however, put forward any arguments whatever. Some constraints of public reason are appropriate and binding.

Despite my disagreement with Rawls, I am prepared to go a good deal further with him than those critics who seem to reject public reason altogether. To see just how far I am willing to go, it is helpful to think of Rawls's argument as proceeding in three stages. The first concludes that citizens who advocate policies bearing on constitutional essentials and matters of basic justice are required to show how they can be supported by a reasonable balance of political values. Political values are drawn from conceptions of political justice. The second stage lays out and defends features those conceptions must have if they are to furnish values adequate for conducting public political argument about these matters. The third, on which Rawls spends relatively little time, illustrates the second by showing how a balance of values drawn from Rawls's own conception of justice might settle questions of basic justice and the constitutional essentials.

I shall not discuss the third stage at all. Instead I suggest that the argument of the first stage is correct and I focus on only the most important of the features isolated at the second, the one that does the most work. That feature, I suggest, is too strong and depends upon a conception of citizenship that I question. To distinguish the stages of the argument clearly and to raise questions about them, I attempt to regiment the argument as strictly as possible. The regimentation of the argument that results is, I believe, faithful to what Rawls has in mind, but its strictness comes at a price. For one thing, it freezes in place a treatment of the issue that Rawls continues to develop and that therefore remains somewhat fluid. For another, the argument as I present it uses theses Rawls defends in the course of discussing other topics, theses whose connection to this argument I shall have to make explicit. Because I have to combine premises and lines of thought from different part of Rawls's work, there is no one passage that I can reproduce here and whose argument I can claim to be reconstructing. I therefore assume a basic familiarity with the relevant texts and draw from them as needed.

The Argument for Observing Public Reason

I suggested earlier that what is at stake in debates about public reason are questions about the most appropriate conception of citizenship for contemporary liberal democracies like the United States. Rawls's own conclusions about public reason turn crucially on his conception of citizenship, which he considers relational. To be a citizen is to stand in a certain relationship to others and to social institutions. He writes:

> (1) the "fundamental political relation of citizenship has two special features: first, it is a relation of citizens within the basic structure of society, a structure we enter only by birth and exit only by death; and second, it is a relation of free and equal citizens who exercise ultimate political power as a collective body."[16]

From *A Theory of Justice* it is clear that the basic structure of society distributes the primary goods—rights, liberties, opportunities, income, wealth, and the social bases of self-respect. So it follows that

> (2) the "fundamental political relation of citizenship" is "a relation of citizens" within a structure that distributes primary goods.

Defending his decision to take the basic structure as the primary subject of justice, Rawls says that "the institutions of the basic structure have deep and long-term social effects and in fundamental ways shape citizens' character and aims, the kinds of persons they are and aspire to be."[17] Citizens' character, aims, and aspirations are the result of their development and exercise of the two moral powers Rawls attributes to citizens: the capacity for a sense of justice and the ability to form, pursue, and revise a conception of the good. The basic structure is able to shape citizens' character so profoundly because the way it distributes primary goods has a profound effect on their ability to develop and exercise their moral powers. That effect is in practice inescapable, since it can be evaded only by death. So:

(3) The way the basic structure distributes primary goods has a profound and inescapable effect on each citizen's ability to develop and exercise her moral powers.

The basic structure includes all of society's basic institutions and not just its governmental ones. Its distributive operations are determined in significant part by what the laws and the constitution permit and prohibit. In what follows I focus exclusively on these determinants since they are the objects of the public deliberations that are supposed to be governed by the guidelines of public reason. For present purposes, I therefore assume that

(4) Laws concerning basic justice and laws and amendments concerning the essential provisions of the Constitution determine the way the basic structure distributes the primary goods.

From (3) and (4) it follows that

(5) Laws concerning basic justice and laws and amendments concerning the essential provisions of the Constitution have a profound and inescapable effect on each citizen's ability to develop and exercise her moral powers.

In *Political Liberalism* Rawls notes that

(6) Citizens "as a collective body, exercise final political and coercive power over one another in enacting laws and amending their constitution."[18]

(5) and (6) together imply that:

(7) The way citizens exercise final political and coercive power as a collective body when the constitutional essentials or matters of basic justice are at stake has a profound and inescapable effect on each citizen's ability to develop and exercise her moral powers.

Democratic theory is committed to the view that citizens are free and equal. This commitment implies, Rawls says, that

(8) "citizens as free and equal have an equal share in the corporate political and coercive power of society."[19]

This implies that when citizens exercise final political power as a collective body in situaitons in which the constitutional essentials or matters of basic justice are at stake, they are equally exercising the political and coercive power of each. From this implication, together with (7), it follows that

(9) Whenever citizens exercise final political and coercive power as a collective body in situations in which the constitutional essentials or matters of basic justice are at stake, they are exercising the political and coercive power of each to produce a profound and inescapable effect on each citizen's ability to develop and exercise her moral powers.

There may be many times in our lives, both extended and episodic, when we are subject to exercises of power that have profound and inescapable effects on the development and exercise of our moral powers. This is particularly so in childhood, when we are subject to parental and pedagogical authorities, as well as to communal authorities of various kinds. The distinguishing mark of citizens' subjection to political power is that in that case, citizens are subject to power which is their own and of which, as we have seen, they are said to have an equal share.[20] When they are subject to laws and a constitution that affect their lives profoundly by determining the distribution of primary goods, they are subject to power that is theirs, exercised in their name and on their authority. When their own power is exercised over them so that it profoundly and inescapably shapes their lives, citizens—considered as free and equal—should be able to affirm the way that power is exercised. To exercise it in these circumstances to enact measures that some citizens could not affirm as free equals is, in effect, to deny them their status as free and equal coholders of their society's political power. This, Rawls would assert, should never be done. And so he would maintain that:

(10) Each citizen, considered as a free and equal coholder of her society's ultimate political power, must be able to affirm the exercise of her own political and coercive power over her to enact measures that have a profound and inescapable effect on her ability to exercise her moral powers.

Citizens need not actually register their approval or affirmation of even the most fundamental exercises of political power. Rather, Rawls thinks that it is both necessary and sufficient if those exercises are such that citizens as such *could* or *would* approve of them. It is both required and enough if those exercises can be justified to them as free equals. That is, Rawls thinks

(11) Each citizen can affirm the exercise of her own political and coercive power over her to enact measures that have a profound and inescapable effect on her ability to exercise her moral powers if and only if the measures enacted are justifiable to her, considered as a free and equal coholder of society's final political power.

From (10) and (11) it follows that

(12) Whenever someone's own political and coercive power is exercised over her to enact measures that have a profound and inescap-

able effect on her ability to develop and exercise her moral powers, the measures enacted must be justifiable to her, considered as a free and equal coholder of that power.

(9) and (12) together imply that

(13) Whenever citizens exercise their ultimate political power as a collective body in situations in which the constitutional essentials or matters of basic justice are at stake, the measures enacted must be justifiable to each, considered as a free and equal coholder of that power.

Since the people exercise their power through a governing apparatus specified by the constitution, (13) implies that

(14) Whenever the government exercises the power of the people in situations in which the constitutional essentials and matters of basic justice are at stake, the measures enacted must be justifiable to each, considered as a free and equal coholder of that power.

An account of public reason is an account of the kind of reasons and inferences that are necessary and sufficient to show that such exercises of power are justifiable to free and equal citizens. Such an account specifies the reasons that governmental officials must use to justify their exercise of power on the most fundamental political questions. When government officials honor the guidelines of public reason, they treat citizens as coholders of their society's power. They thereby put the relationship between the government and the governed on what is, from the point of view of democratic theory, the proper footing. But Rawls says, "the idea of public reason specifies at the deepest level the basic moral and political values that are to determine a constitutional democratic government's relation to its citizens *and their relation to one another*."[21] I indicated earlier that I am interested in the conduct of, and hence the relations among, citizens who are not public officials. As we shall see, the claims Rawls draws on to establish (14) ground his claims about those relations as well.

His argument for those claims depends upon the importance of political arguments offered by ordinary citizens in the public forum. In the various forms of that discourse—questioning candidates for public office, explaining their own votes, speaking in public meetings or in other public deliberative fora—citizens who advocate positions on the constitutional essentials and matters of basic justice publicly evince their will[22] that that position be adopted. More precisely,

(15) When a citizen argues in the public forum for a policy or principles bearing on the constitutional essentials or matters of basic justice, she thereby evinces her will in the public forum that citizens exercise their final political power as a collective body according to her policy or proposal with respect to a matter of basic justice or the constitutional essentials.

From (13) and (15) it follows that

(16) When a citizen argues in the public forum for a policy or principles bearing on the constitutional essentials or matters of basic justice, she thereby evinces her will in the public forum that citizens exercise their final political power as a collective body; the measures enacted must be justifiable to each citizen, considered as a free and equal coholder of society's ultimate political and coercive power.

Suppose that a citizen evinces her will in the public forum that a policy be adopted that must be justifiable to each citizen as a free and equal coholder of society's ultimate power. Suppose further that she is not prepared to show how it can be so justified. And let us understand "preparation" broadly, so that someone is unprepared to do this only if she expresses no interest in showing how her position could be justified in this way, does not know how it could be shown and expresses no interest in learning how it could be, is dismissive of requests that she show it, and attaches no significance to the fact that her interlocutors do try to justify the principles and policies they advocate. Then her interlocutors could reasonably believe she thinks the policy should be adopted regardless of whether it is justifiable to each. Now recall that when citizens exercise final political power as a collective body in situations in which the constitutional essentials or matters of basic justice are at stake, they are equally exercising the political and coercive power of each. It follows that

(17) If a citizen evinces her will in the public forum that citizens exercise their ultimate political power as a collective body and the measures enacted must be justifiable to each citizen, considered as a free and equal coholder of society's final political and coercive power, and she is not prepared to show how it can be so justified, then she evinces her will that citizens exercise the political and coercive power of each citizen regardless of whether it is justifiable to each in this way.

(17), together with (9) and (11), implies that

(18) If a citizen evinces her will in the public forum that citizens exercise their final political power as a collective body regardless of whether it is justifiable to each citizen and the constitutional essentials or matters of basic justice are at stake, then she evinces her will that citizens exercise the political and coercive power of each citizen to enact measures some may be unable to affirm in situations in which it has a profound and inescapable effect on the ability of citizens to develop and exercise their moral powers.

Earlier I said that when a citizen's own power is exercised over her so that it profoundly and inescapably shapes her life, she should be able to affirm the measures enacted. To enact measures they could not affirm as free equals is, in effect, to deny them their status as free and equal coholders of their society's political power. This, together with (18), implies that

(19) If a citizen evinces her will in the public forum that citizens exercise their final political power as a collective body to enact measures that are not justifiable to each citizen in situations in which the constitutional essentials or matters of basic justice are at stake,

then she evinces her will in the public forum that citizens adopt her proposal even if this entails failing to treat some as free and equal coholders of society's final political power.

If the citizens who behave in this way are very influential or very numerous, their interlocutors could well doubt whether the constitutional essential or matter of basic justice at issue will be settled consistent with the status of each as a free and equal coholder of society's ultimate political power. Rawls thinks that what he calls the "fundamental political relation of citizenship" should be characterized by mutual trust and respect of citizens as such. Citizens should be able to trust that all want everyone to be treated as a free and equal coholder of their society's final power when fundamental matters are at stake. They should also respect one another as persons who should be so treated. So even if the citizens who do what (19) describes are neither influential nor numerous, their conduct can undermine this mutual trust and respect. In sum,

(20) If a citizen evinces her will in the public forum that citizens exercise their final political power as a collective body regardless of whether the measures are justifiable to each citizen in situations in which the constitutional essentials or matters of basic justice are at stake, she can threaten the possibility that all will believe these issues will be settled consistent with the status of each as a free and equal coholder of society's final political power and threaten the "fundamental political relation of citizenship" by undermining mutual trust, mutual respect and civic friendship.

(16), (17), and (20) imply the cumbersome

(21) When a citizen argues in the public forum for a policy or principles bearing on the constitutional essentials or matters of basic justice and she is not prepared to show how the measures she advocates can be justified to each as a free and equal coholder of society's final political power, she can threaten the possibility that all will believe the constitutional essentials and matters of basic justice are settled consistent with the status of each as a free and

equal coholder of society's ultimate political power and threaten the "fundamental political relation of citizenship" by undermining mutual trust, mutual respect, and civic friendship.

Rawls remarks at one point that the values of civility are very great values, not lightly to be abandoned. So, suppose Rawls would endorse:

(22) Because it is a very great good that all believe the constitutional essentials and matters of basic justice are settled consistent with the status of each as a free and equal coholder of society's final political power and that the "fundamental political relation of citizenship" be characterized by mutual trust, mutual respect, and civic friendship, citizens ought not act in ways that undermine these.

(21) and (22) imply

(23) When a citizen argues in the public forum for a policy or principles bearing on the constitutional essentials or matters of basic justice, she should be prepared to show how it can be justified to each as a free and equal coholder of society's final political power.

In a famous passage in *Political Liberalism*, Rawls puts forward what he calls "the liberal principle of legitimacy." This principle lays out the conditions under which exercises of power are justifiable to citizens as such. According to the liberal principle of legitimacy, "our exercise of political power is proper and hence justifiable only when it is exercised in accordance with a constitution the essentials of which all citizens may reasonably be expected to endorse in light of principles and ideals acceptable to them as reasonable and rational."[23] This principle, together with (23), implies

(24) When a citizen argues in the public forum for a policy or principles bearing on the constitutional essentials or matters of basic justice, she should be prepared to show that the principle or policy she advocates is in accordance with a constitution the essentials of

which all citizens may reasonably be expected to endorse in light of principles and ideals acceptable to them as reasonable and rational.

What principles and ideals can citizens reasonably be expected to endorse as reasonable and rational? How can some citizens show others that the policies they advocate are in accordance with a constitution whose essentials embody those principles and ideals? Here, I believe, Rawls would reply that

(25) A principle or policy bearing on the constitutional essentials is in accordance with a constitution the essentials of which all citizens may reasonably be expected to endorse in light of principles and ideals acceptable to them as reasonable and rational only if it can be supported by a reasonable balance of political values.

(24) and (25) entail the conclusion Rawls famously reaches in *Political Liberalism*:[24]

(26) When a citizen argues in the public forum for a policy or principles bearing on the constitutional essentials or matters of basic justice, she should be prepared to show "on those fundamental questions how the principles and policies they advocate and vote for can be supported by [a reasonable balance of] the political values of public reason."

Rawls echoes this conclusion later when he remarks, "what public reason asks is that citizens be able to explain their votes to one another in terms of a reasonable balance of public political values."[25] This reconstruction therefore shows how Rawls might reach just the conclusions about public reason that he explicitly endorses on the basis of other claims that he makes. There is good reason to think that it captures the argument he had in mind.

The Duties of Public Reason as Role-Specific Duties

An especially puzzling feature of the argument is that while (26) purports to express a moral obligation, it is remarkably elusive about the ground of that requirement. Requirements governing the way citizens are to treat one another enter the argument at step (22). Principle (22) says that citizens ought not undermine mutual trust, respect, civic friendship, or a generally held belief that the constitutional essentials and matters of basic justice are settled consistent with each citizen's status. I imputed to Rawls the claim that they ought not do this because friendship, respect, trust, and the prevalence of this belief are "very great goods." I did so because, in a crucial passage explaining why citizens are obliged to honor the guidelines of public reason, Rawls says that "the political values realized by a well-ordered constitutional regime are very great values and not easily overridden and the ideals they express are not to be lightly abandoned."[26] But the fact that values realized by honoring public reason are "very great values" does not entail that citizens in "a well-ordered constitutional regime" are *required* to honor the guidelines. Even if they are, it does not follow that *we* are required to follow them.[27]

Perhaps honoring public reason is part of a moral ideal, conformity with which is supererogatory for citizens of a well-ordered society or for us. This thought gains some support from a remark Rawls makes in a passage that occurs shortly before the one I just quoted. There he says:

> As reasonable and rational, and knowing that they affirm a diversity of reasonably religious and philosophical doctrines, they should be ready to explain the basis of their actions to one another in terms each could reasonably expect that others might endorse as consistent with their freedom and equality. Trying to meet this condition is one of the tasks that the ideal of democratic politics asks of us.[28]

Yet Rawls also associates a related ideal with a moral requirement, saying that "the ideal of citizenship imposes a moral, not a legal, duty—the duty of civility," a duty citizens perform when they honor the requirements of public reason.[29] The problem with this remark is that it is not at all obvious how moral ideals can impose moral requirements. Let us think of the ideal of citizenship as an abstract conception of a citizen who realizes to a perfect or an exemplary degree all of the excellences associated with that role. It may well be that we instantiate very great goods when we realize that ideal. It may also be that we can realize that ideal only if we comply with the guidelines of public reason. This implies that it is in some way good to comply with those guidelines, but not that we are required to do so.

The morality of ideals is an important but neglected and ill-understood part of ethics.[30] It overlaps but is not congruent with the morality of roles, which I take to be concerned with norms and requirements governing the adequate performance of personal and social roles. One way to get from the ideal of citizenship to the duties of civility would be to deflate the notion of an ideal so as to narrow the difference between the two. Then the ideal of citizenship might be understood merely as a conception of a citizen who perfectly honors her role-specific duties. With a description of the ideal in hand, we could work backwards to the role-specific duties of citizenship. If those role-specific duties could be shown to include the duty of civility and if that, in turn, could be shown to include the duty to abide by the guidelines of public reason, then the ideal of citizenship might be said to impose the requirement to honor those guidelines, as Rawls suggests it does.

This attempt to derive requirements from ideals goes wrong in two ways. First, the attempt depends upon a deflation of ideals that makes them too flat. Though I cannot pursue this matter here, I believe it mistaken to think of personal ideals as exemplifying no moral excellences beyond a propensity to perform one's duty, or one's role-specific duty, perfectly. Deflating ideals allows the part they play in the moral life to escape. Second, this line of thought includes an unnecessary shuffle. It must begin with a conception of citizenship and the associated role-specific duties in order to elaborate a conception of the citizen who performs those duties ideally. It must then read the role-specific duties back off the ideal in order to salvage the claim that it is the ideal that imposes them. It would be both more economical and more philosophically defensible to specify, not the *ideal* of citizenship with its attendant excellences, but the *role* of citizenship in a "constitutional democratic society." Specifying this role could also include the articulation of role-specific duties, such as the duty expressed in (26). This would enable Rawls to bypass (22) and claim that (26) expresses a role-specific duty arrived at via

(22′) Citizens in liberal democracies are under role-specific duties not to threaten mutual trust, mutual respect, civic friendship, and the generally held belief that the constitutional essentials and matters of basic justice are settled consistent with the status of each as a free and equal coholder of society's final political power.

Proceeding this way would allow Rawls to take the difference between the morality of roles and the morality of ideals seriously. It would allow him to claim that citizens in an ideally ordered society realize the ideal of citizenship by exemplifying all of the excellences associated with that role. It would allow him to claim that the ideal of citizenship, as realized in a well-ordered society, can play an important motivational role once his theory is introduced into contemporary philosophical and political cultures.[31] It would further allow him to claim that his ideal plays this role by eliciting in actual citizens a conception-dependent desire to pursue the ideal themselves.[32] Finally, it would allow him to claim that (26) expresses a requirement and it would allow him to do so without claiming that the ideal imposes it.

In what follows I impute the revised argument to Rawls. I suppose, that is, that he means to derive the requirements of public reason from claims about the morality of roles rather than the morality of ideals and that the obligation purportedly expressed in (26) is supported by (22′) rather than (22). Of course this interpretation raises problems of its own. Liberal societies typically contain a vast number of secondary associations.[33] Their citizens typically occupy a number of roles, the demands of which may conflict. We need to know how to adjudicate those conflicts, including conflicts between the demands of citizenship and those of other roles. Furthermore, specifying the role of citizenship and its duties requires making certain assumptions about the educational, economic, political, and epistemic conditions of those who will typically or ideally occupy the role. There will be difficult questions about those of whom the assumptions are false. Citizens who have been denied the education they would need to comply with the guidelines of public reason provide a ready source of counterexamples to the claim that anyone who violates them has done something morally exceptionable. But it would be premature to seize on these conflicts and counterexamples as proof that Rawls's treatment of public reason is in error. The prior question is: Do the role-specific duties of citizenship in actual "constitutional democratic societ[ies]" like the United States include the duty to comply with (26)? Only if the answer is yes need we go on to ask whether the demands of citizenship trump the demands of our other roles and whether putative counterexamples can be explained away.

Rawls clearly thinks the answer is yes. He would be right in thinking so if he could claim to have specified the role of citizenship in a way that is correct or most reasonable for our society. To see whether he is, note first that this specification involves a description, not just of the powers citizens have as such, but also of the interests, expectations, and activities normally expected of citizens who fulfill their social role adequately. If that specification is to be appropriate for us, then it must be that we are or should attempt to become citizens who engage in those activities, are moved by those interests, and attach to them the importance Rawls thinks we should. Asking whether a given conception of citizenship is appropriate for us entails asking about whether we should try to conform ourselves and our interests to that conception.

"The Proviso"

Principle (26) says that a citizen arguing in the public forum when constitutional essentials are at stake should be prepared to show

how her position can be supported by a reasonable balance of political values. Leaving aside thorny questions about reasonability, I take it what Rawls has in mind is this: The political is a realm of human affairs analytically distinguishable from other realms of human life. Corresponding to that realm is a set of moral values that can be realized only by political institutions and in political relations among citizens and nations, though analogous values can be realized elsewhere. Examples of political values, Rawls says, are "those mentioned in the preamble to the United States Constitution: a more perfect union, justice, domestic tranquillity, the common defense, the general welfare and the blessings of liberty."[34] Political matters, or at least the most important of them, ought not be settled without appeal to values proper to the political realm. And so, as (25) implies, citizens should be expected to endorse a settlement of these matters only if that settlement can be justified by appealing to a reasonable balance of political values. Citizens, Rawls concludes in (26), should be prepared to show how the positions they publicly advocate and vote for can be supported by such a balance.

Principle (26) has been widely discussed. It has been criticized by those who think that participatory democracy requires allowing marginalized citizens to introduce any arguments they like into public deliberation.[35] It has been criticized as well by those who think citizens should be able to introduce their religious views into political argument.[36] These are criticisms Rawls hastens to disarm by pointing out that the introduction of what he calls "comprehensive doctrine" into public political argument concerning the constitutional essentials and matters of basic justice is compatible with satisfying the requirement expressed by (26). In a passage expressing what he calls "the proviso," he writes: "This requirement still allows us to introduce into political discussion at any time our comprehensive doctrine, religious or nonreligious, provided that, in due course, we give properly public reasons to support the principles and policies our comprehensive doctrine is said to support."[37] Thus if someone wants to argue against the legality of abortion or assisted suicide, (26) allows him to argue that these acts show impious disregard for the sanctity of innocent human life. But he must also be prepared to show that such disregard offends against political justice and the proper ends of political society.

One of the advances of modernity, anticipated to be sure by many thinkers in the premodern period, is the recognition that human life is differentiated. Modernity is characterized by the general recognition that human life can be distinguished into diverse spheres of activity in which different kinds of values—political, economic, aesthetic, religious, and so on—are to be pursued and realized.[38] One of the lingering philosophical problems of modernity—call it "the modernist problem"—is that of how these spheres of life and their associated families of values are to be organized into a coherent whole. The powerful distributive role of the modern nation state and its claim to a monopoly on justified coercion give it enormous power to shape lives and secondary associations. In modern democracies, the state enjoys this power at the same time that it can be swayed by politically powerful private organizations. This raises a particularly acute form of the modernist problem: How are the values proper to the political realm related to those proper to other realms of human life? Rawls gives a partial answer to that lingering problem, arguing that democratic citizens should be able to see the conception of justice realized in the political life of their society as consistent with but standing free of other moral values.

Rawls may or may not be correct about this, as he may or may not be correct that mutual trust, respect, and friendship depend upon appealing to them. But he is surely correct to make the modernist assertion that the political constitutes an analytically distinguishable sphere of human life in which intrinsic values of a distinct kind are realized. It is on the basis of these values—values such as the common good, the liberty of citizens, political equality—that the most fundamental political issues are properly settled. Among the qualities democracy demands of citizens is the ability to reason with others about those issues. And so I think

Rawls is correct to say, as he does in (26), that when fundamental matters are at stake citizens should be prepared to show how the positions they advocate and vote for can be supported by a balance of political values. Though I cannot argue the point here, I would add that to be a citizen is to be member of a society that has a political common good or public interest. To be a citizen of a democracy is to belong to a political society the members of which are in some sense equal. Doing one's part as a citizen requires according the demands of the common good and political equality a central place in reasoning about fundamental political matters. I therefore think that citizens of a democracy must, as a matter of role-specific duty, be prepared to justify their positions on those questions by appealing to a balance of political values among which the common good or the public interest of equal citizens occupies a central place. It is appropriate to think of citizens of liberal democracies such as the United States as having a role-specific interest in receiving such justification from one another, and it would be appropriate for them to have or develop the expectation of receiving them.

The role-specific duty I have isolated is relatively weak. Someone who argues for school prayer on the grounds that society will flourish only if its children are brought up to worship God satisfies this duty, since the flourishing of society is a political value. Furthermore, as I indicated earlier, some might be exempt from the role-specific duty governing their arguments. Perhaps there are some who, because of their circumstances, need not be prepared to appeal to the common good or to political values at all. But to grant that is not to admit that the duty I have identified is not a role-specific one. It is merely to note that some citizens may be so circumstanced that their role-specific duties are overridden.

Rawls's "proviso" might seem more problematic. It is not clear what he means by "in due course," as he readily acknowledges. He does not explain why prevalence of the belief that citizens will satisfy (26) is sufficient for the trust, respect and civic friendship referred to in (21). Why, we might wonder, doesn't the resort to other, nonpolitical reasons undermine these, particularly if the reasons that really seem to move us are *not* political values? Offering disrespectful arguments to our interlocutors can damage other relationships even if we subsequently add respectful ones. Will this not damage the relationship among citizens as well?[39] Rawls might reply that citizenship is different from other relationships in which individuals exercise power over one another.[40] The trust, respect, and friendship that should obtain among citizens in a liberal democracy are therefore analogous to, rather than identical with, the trust, respect, and friendship that ought to obtain among parties to, say, familial or commercial relationships. These differences entail differences in the conditions necessary and sufficient for maintaining the relationship's quality. There is a limit to what we can learn about those conditions by looking at family or professional life. Indeed, Rawls might continue, to begin with a notion of mutual respect drawn from private life and ask whether it can be maintained in politics by complying with (26) is to go at things the wrong way. Rather, we should work back and forth, modifying our notion of reasonable public political argument in light of our intuitions about respect at the same time that we modify our intuitions about respect in light of what seems, on reflection, the most reasonable standard of public political argument.

Claims about the interests citizens have as such, and the importance they attach to them, are crucial to Rawls's argument for (26). To see this, note that regimenting Rawls's argument helps to explain an especially interesting feature of his treatment of public reason. Citizens, he suggests in one place, should ask themselves how their contributions to public debate would be received if they were included in a Supreme Court opinion. Elsewhere he says that "our exercise of political power is proper only when we sincerely believe that the reasons we offer for our political actions—*were we to state them as government officials*—are sufficient, and we also reasonably think that other citizens might also reasonably accept those reasons."[41] Rawls endorses these tests because he accepts (6), according to which citizens are thought of as coholders of their society's final power, a power judges and other government officials exercise on their behalf. Thus, because Rawls accepts (6), he also thinks that in the instances of justification referred to in (14) and (23)—the justification which a citizen can expect of her government when fundamental matters are at issue and that which she must be prepared to offer others in the same cases—those to whom the justification is offered should be thought of in the same way, as coholders of their society's final power. This is an important consequence. It, via (25) and the liberal principle of legitimacy, enables Rawls to arrive at the claim that both instances of justification should appeal to political values. Recall now that according to (21), when citizens are not prepared to offer one another justifications of the right sort, they can threaten the quality of the "political relationship of citizenship." The relationship can be threatened only if citizens have a role-specific interest in the kind of justification others are prepared to offer them and a corresponding role-specific expectation that they will receive it. It can be threatened, that is, only if citizens have a role-specific expectation that others will comply with (26). If this conception of citizenship is appropriate for the United States, then the expectation that others comply with (26) is one that American citizens should have or develop. Rawls ultimately thinks we should have or develop it because he thinks the conception of citizenship expressed by (6) is appropriate for us.

So far I have indicated agreement with the conclusions of the first stage of Rawls's argument. But (26) and the proviso require more of citizens than I have suggested so far. They require not only that citizens justify their positions on fundamental questions in due course by appeal to political values, but that those values be *the political values of public reason*. The qualification adds that these values and the principles used to strike a balance among them must be drawn from one or another conception of justice with certain distinctive features. Seeing what those features are takes us to the second stage of Rawls's argument. It is there that I shall raise questions, asking whether one of the requirements Rawls imposes on conceptions of justice is too strong for the contemporary United States and asks citizens to cultivate interests and expectations which they need not develop under current conditions. We have already seen that (6) is crucial to the argument for (26). It is crucial to Rawls's arguments for that condition as well. The strength of the condition is ultimately due, I shall suggest, to reliance on an interpretation of (6) that is inappropriately strong.

The Features of Political Conception and the Content of Public Reason

"The content of public reason," Rawls says, "is given by the principles and values of the family of liberal political conceptions of justice meeting these conditions":

First, their principles apply to basic political and social institutions (the basic structure of society);
Second, they can be presented independently from comprehensive doctrines of any kind (although they may, of course, be supported by a reasonable overlapping consensus of such doctrines); and
Finally, they can be worked out from fundamental ideas as seen implicit in the public political culture of a constitutional regime, such as the conceptions of citizens as free and equal persons, and of society as a fair system of cooperation.[42]

Liberal political conceptions, he says, are characterized by "three main features":

First, a list of certain basic rights, liberties and opportunities (such as those familiar from constitutional regimes);
Second, an assignment of special priority to those rights, liberties and opportunities, especially with respect to the claims of the general good and perfectionist values; and
Third, measures ensuring for all citizens adequate all-purpose means to make effective use of their freedoms.[43]

These remarks, together with (26), imply that when a citizen argues in the public forum for a policy or principles bearing on the constitutional essentials or matters of basic justice, she should be prepared to show how those principles or policies can be supported by a reasonable balance of political values drawn from conceptions of justice with these six features. Summing up, Rawls writes, "to engage in public reason is to appeal to one of these political conceptions—to their ideals and principles, standards and values—when debating fundamental political questions."[44]

I shall not comment on the three features that distinguish liberal from nonliberal political conceptions. Nor shall I take up the first and third of the three conditions that together single out liberal conceptions that can serve as sources of the political values of public reason. Instead I want to focus on the second, which I take to be the most important. Without it, citizens could resort to conceptions of political justice that are based upon, or that they think are based upon, comprehensive doctrine. It is this possibility that the second condition is designed to rule out. While this condition does not entail that citizens ought not appeal to the natural law or to biblical conceptions of justice, say, it does entail that such appeals are not unimpeachable as they stand. Citizens should always be prepared to go further and show how the principles they employ can be grounded in a freestanding conception of political justice. Given this implication, it is hard to overstate the importance of the second condition. Indeed it this condition that I believe many critics really mean to object to when they reject the quite different claim, which I endorsed, that policies should be justified by appeal to a balance of political values.[45]

The independence at issue in the second condition is evidential. To say that a conception can be presented as being independent of comprehensive doctrine is to say it can be presented as a conception that is acceptable without the evidential support of comprehensive doctrine. Now consider someone whose conception of justice centers on the notion of a national common good. Suppose she thinks the common good of the United States can be realized only if the laws forbid activities that are especially inimical to genuine human flourishing. She recognizes that others share many of the principles of justice that she endorses. But she also accepts principles about the scope of rights and liberties that would be accepted only by those who accept her views about the human good. Suppose, for example, that she would publicly argue against recognizing a right to assisted suicide because she thinks it wrong to choose death over life and because she thinks societies lose something of great ethical significance when they regard the moment of death as subject to individual control. Suppose further that there are no other compelling reasons for prohibiting assisted suicide.[46] Such a person proposes settling a fundamental constitutional question by appealing to political principles drawn from a conception of justice that cannot be presented independent of comprehensive doctrine. Why has she violated a role-specific duty of citizenship?

Rawls would begin by pointing to two facts about liberal democracies. One is what he calls "the fact of pluralism":

(27) Liberal democracies are characterized by deep and enduring disagreement about comprehensive doctrine.

The other is what he calls "the fact of oppression"[47]:

(28) This disagreement can be eliminated in the long run only by the oppressive use of state power.

These two facts imply that there is deep and enduring disagreement about the comprehensive doctrine on which our agent's conception of justice depends, a disagreement that can be eliminated in the long run only by the oppressive use of state power. Her conception provides the grounds for political principles forbidding the legalization of assisted suicide. The political question at stake in the example is a fundamental one, and hence one with special bearing on citizens' ability to develop and exercise their moral powers. Therefore

(29) There is deep and enduring disagreement about the comprehensive doctrine needed to support principles enjoining citizens to exercise the political and coercive power of each to produce a profound and inescapable effect on each citizen's ability to develop and exercise her moral powers, a disagreement which can be eliminated only by the oppressive use of state power.

I am supposing that our agent's comprehensive doctrine provides the only grounds on which it is reasonable to accept a principle forbidding assisted suicide. Others can accept those principles only if they accept her comprehensive doctrine, or the parts of it needed to support those principles. So (29) implies that

(30) Citizens can be brought to agree on principles enjoining them to exercise the political and coercive power of each to produce a profound and inescapable effect on each citizen's ability to develop and exercise her moral powers and which depend on that comprehensive doctrine, only by the oppressive use of state power.

The oppressive use of state power is, by definition, a use of state power that at least some citizens cannot affirm as free and equal coholders of society's power. By (8) it is a use of the power of each that at least some cannot affirm. Therefore the use of state power to bring about agreement on principles forbidding the legalization of assisted suicide is a use of the power of each that at least some cannot affirm as free and equal coholders of their society's ultimate political power. So

(31) Citizens, considered as free and equal coholders of society's final political power, cannot affirm principles which enjoin them to exercise the political and coercive power of each to produce a profound and inescapable effect on each citizen's ability to develop and exercise her moral powers and which depend upon comprehensive doctrine.

This, taken together with (11), implies that

(32) Principles which enjoin citizens to exercise the political and coercive powers of each to produce a profound and inescapable effect on each citizen's ability to develop and exercise her moral powers, and which depend upon comprehensive doctrine, are not justifiable to each, considered as a free and equal coholder of society's final political power.

(9), (15), and (32) imply that

(33) When a citizen argues in the public forum for a policy or principles bearing on the constitutional essentials or matters of basic justice, and those principles depend upon comprehensive doctrine, she thereby evinces her will in the public forum that citizens exercise their final political power as a collective body according to a policy or principles which is not justifiable to each, considered as a free and equal coholder of society's final power.

(21) and (33) imply that

(34) When a citizen argues in the public forum for a policy or principles bearing on the constitutional essentials or matters of basic justice, and those principles depend upon comprehensive doctrine, she thereby threatens the possibility that all will believe the constitutional essentials and matters of basic justice are settled consistent with the status of each as a free and equal coholder of society's final political power and threatens the "fundamental political relation of citizenship" by undermining mutual trust and mutual respect.

Finally, (22) and (34) imply

(35) When a citizen argues in the public forum for a policy or principles bearing on the constitutional essentials or matters of basic justice, and those principles depend upon comprehensive doctrine, she does something she should not.

And so Rawls would conclude that

(36) When a citizen argues in the public forum for a policy or principles bearing on the constitutional essentials or matters of basic

justice, she should be prepared to defend her position by appeal to principles drawn from a conception of justice that can be presented as being independent of comprehensive doctrine.

Some questions might be raised about (27) and (28), the facts of pluralism and of oppression. Moreover, the move from (29) to (30) might be suspect. It seems to ignore the possibilities that agents could reasonably accept the political principles in question without any basis at all or could accept them as self-evidently true. But while these are real possibilities, taking them too seriously renders the condition on conceptions of justice trivial. Any conception of justice could be presented as being independent of comprehensive doctrine if we were to suppose that it could be accepted as self-evident. The most interesting step in the argument, and the one I want to examine, is (34). It is by supporting (34) that the strong interpretation of (6) comes into play.

Some Difficulties with Public Reason

Principle (34) says that when fundamental matters are at stake, publicly appealing to principles which can be justified only by appeal to comprehensive doctrine threatens mutual trust and respect. I mentioned earlier that Rawls thinks of the political domain as a distinct one in which irreducibly political values are realized. This suggests that the trust and respect that ought to characterize relations among citizens, and that (22') says citizens should try to maintain, are forms of trust and respect distinctive to the political realm, as Rawls understands it. If this is so, then the trust and respect referred to in (34), the trust and respect threatened by appeal to principles justifiable only on the basis of comprehensive doctrine, must have features that distinguish it from trust and respect of other sorts. Thus (34) is compatible with the claim that there are some forms of mutual trust and respect that are not threatened by the invocation of comprehensive doctrine. If there are, then the reason for singling out the forms that are threatened in (34), and for asserting in (22') that citizens are obligated not to threaten them, must be that those are the forms of mutual trust and respect most appropriate for citizens of a pluralistic liberal democracy. This, I believe, is Rawls's view. To show that it is, I want to turn to an example that he himself discusses.

Rawls says of Martin Luther King, Jr. that his use of religious language was not unreasonable because he would have been willing to justify his position on civil rights in the public forum by appeal to the values of public reason. This is crucial if Rawls is to avoid implying that King violated a moral requirement by arguing for civil rights as he did. But why think that trust in and respect for King depends upon the belief that he would have defended the positions he did in the public forum by appealing to a conception of justice that is independent of comprehensive doctrine?

To pursue this question, I want to ask two others. Why we are so ready to believe that King would have followed the guidelines of public reason had his reasonability been in question? And why was he not called upon to do it, supposing for the sake of argument that he was not? It seems clear that the civil rights policies that King advocated could be supported by a conception of justice that does not depend upon religious premises. But the obviousness of the fact that they could have been cannot explain why King was not called upon to show how they could be, and this for two reasons. One is that it is possible for people to act from the wrong motives in adducing religious arguments for policies that can be supported in that way. It is surely possible for someone to endorse policies that can be so supported, but to do so with total disregard for what other citizens could reasonably be expected to endorse. And so it is possible that King adduced religious arguments for civil rights measures with total disregard for whether others could regard him as reasonable. Furthermore, while it now seems obvious that King's positions could be supported by a conception of justice that does not depend upon comprehensive doctrine, this is because he was so successful in convincing people that his cause was just. But that he could do so using religious arguments is precisely what needs to be explained.

The explanation lies in important facts about American political sociology. The United States is an increasingly pluralistic society. Yet Judeo-Christian ethics, stories, forms of expression, and manifestations of faith are familiar even to those who reject their theological commitments or the distinctive tenets of their various religious moralities. This is due in part to their continuing presence in culture and in part to their historical role in forming American political ideas. Because of this familiarity, those who are not religious or are of differing religious convictions can recognize one another's concern for the common good of all and for the country's future. They can recognize this even when their concern for the common good is expressed in religious language and even when religious language is used to argue for policies with which they profoundly disagree. Furthermore, religious symbols, language, and expressions of faith have the power to move even those who are not religious. While this might be attributed to the residual hold of a rejected faith, I think a more sophisticated explanation is called for. Religion makes meaningful the most common and fundamental human experiences: suffering and death, sin and guilt, repentance, forgiveness and redemption, the experience of injustice and vulnerability, and the hope that right will triumph. The familiarity of certain forms of religion enables those who are not religious to find in religious discourse moral propositions about those experiences with which they concur and which can move them to action. Sometimes this is straightforward enough. At other times it can be found only with sophisticated reinterpretation or misinterpretation of religious argument. Religious people often do the same with their thoroughly secular fellows, interpreting their discourse in what they take to be a charitable way so as to find a basis for agreement. Once such a basis of agreement is found, it is possible for cooperative political action, trust, and respect to flourish even without political argument that avoids comprehensive doctrine.

Citizens do not always look for a basis of agreement in one another's religious political discourse, but they do sometimes and it is interesting to ask why. They did in the case of Martin Luther King.[48] They did so, I believe, because of the moral authority he had in American public life.[49] That authority derived not only from what King said in the public forum, but also from what his fellow citizens believed about his life and the depth of his convictions. It derived as well from what they knew of the suffering of his people and of his own readiness to share those sufferings. What African Americans underwent, and what King was willing to undergo, could be recognized as suffering even by those who did not share King's religious beliefs. His evident willingness to undergo it helped purchase him the authority that enabled him to use religious arguments in the public forum without raising questions about his reasonability. If my suggestions are correct, then reactions to the arguments King made in the public forum depended upon what he did outside it. They also depended upon thinking of King as a member of a racial group that suffered great oppression and injustice.

The example shows that political cooperation, civic friendship, mutual trust, and respect in a pluralistic society sometimes depend upon conceiving one another as members of groups whose history we know, on mutual understanding of familiar comprehensive doctrines, and on recognizing others' moral authority. These, in turn, make it possible for American citizens to recognize when those who appeal to comprehensive doctrine are sincerely committed to the country's ideals and common good as they conceive them. We might think that this is sufficient to explain the prevalence of mutual trust, respect, and civic friendship. Rawls, however, thinks it necessary to go one step further. He thinks trust, respect, and friendship are threatened unless citizens believe others are willing to justify their positions by public reason. This implies, as (34) says, that they are threatened unless citizens believe that Martin Luther King was willing to justify his position by appeal to principles drawn from a conception of the country's ideals and common good that does not depend upon comprehensive doctrine. And so Rawls must claim the example shows only that the conditions of that belief are complex and dependent upon contextual knowledge. Why think the extra step is necessary? Why not deny (34) and opt for the simpler explanation of trust and respect?

These questions can be made more pressing by turning to another example, one Rawls does not discuss. In anticipation of a White House meeting on race to which he had been invited, the great Jewish refugee theologian Abraham Heschel sent an open telegram to President Kennedy. In it, he urged Kennedy to adopt a "Marshall Plan for aid to Negroes." Religious citizens of all faiths should support such a plan, he said, because "[w]e forfeit the right to worship God as long as we continue to humiliate Negroes."[50] I presume what Heschel had in mind was that God requires that we do justice to our fellow citizens and that we do violence to our relationship with God when we do not. Thus Heschel publicly appealed to a religious conception of justice to argue that his fellow citizens should shoulder the burdens of an expensive program for aid to African Americans.

Now suppose for the sake of argument that Heschel would have refused to justify his position in any other terms. Suppose further that he would have refused because, two decades after the Holocaust, he thought it vitally important to keep Jewish social thought alive and he believed this could be done only if American Jews publicly interpreted the demands of justice in distinctively Jewish terms.[51] In this case, as in Martin Luther King's, it seems to me that Heschel would not have threatened mutual trust, respect, and civic friendship. And it seems to me that he would not have for the same reason that King did not. In both their cases, keeping relations with their fellow citizens on the proper footing was a matter of satisfying the valid interests and expectations fellow citizens had of their public political arguments. Heschel, like King, satisfied them by exercising moral authority to lodge a claim of justice on the national conscience. He did so in terms of a familiar comprehensive doctrine that his fellow citizens could interpret to find a basis of agreement. As with King, so with Heschel, the authority his fellow citizens accorded him, and the trust and respect he enjoyed, depended in part upon his activities outside the public forum. And it depended on his being regarded as a member of a group which suffered grave injustice.

Rawls's most recent discussion of public reason might leave room for him to claim that even Heschel would have satisfied (36).[52] But why think that this is what explains the fact that Heschel would not have threatened trust, respect, and civic friendship? Why not opt for the simpler explanation I proposed when discussing Martin Luther King? The answer is that even if Rawls accepts the simpler explanation for the prevalence of some form of trust and respect, he thinks (34) expresses conditions of the forms of trust, respect, and friendship that are most appropriate for citizens of a liberal democracy. Rawls must explain the examples in a way that is consistent with it. The prevalence of the right forms of trust, respect, and friendship depend upon the legitimate interests and expectations of citizens. Therefore Rawls must think that citizens of a liberal democracy are best thought of as having an interest in receiving justifications that do not depend upon comprehensive doctrine when fundamental matters are at stake, and they should expect to receive such justifications from their fellow citizens. If these claims follow from a conception of citizenship that Rawls thinks appropriate for the contemporary United States, then he must think that American citizens have that interest, should hold one another to that expectation, and that the quality of their relationship should depend upon whether they believe they will receive justifications from their fellow citizens that do not depend upon comprehensive doctrine.

To see why Rawls thinks this, recall that (6) is crucial to his argument for (26). It is also crucial, via (9) and (33), for (34). Principle (6) says:

Citizens "as a collective body, exercise final political and coercive power over one another in enacting laws and amending their constitution."

Citizens could exercise "final political power" over one another just in case there is no political authority with the right to reverse the duly expressed decisions of the body of citizens on fundamental political questions. This interpretation is compatible with the claim that citizens' authority to exercise that power depends upon their exercising it in a way that is consistent with an antecedently given moral code. Rawls, however, endorses a stronger interpretation of "final" and hence of (6). In his discussion of political autonomy, Rawls writes:

> How are fair terms of cooperation to be determined? Are they to be simply laid down by some outside authority distinct from the persons cooperating, say by God's law? Or are these terms to be accepted by these persons as fair in view of their knowledge of an independent moral order? Or should these terms be established by an undertaking among those persons themselves in view of what they regard as their reciprocal advantage?
>
> Justice as fairness . . . adopts a form of this last answer.[53]

Thus in saying that citizens exercise "final political power" over one another, Rawls does not mean merely that there is no political power more fundamental than that which citizens exercise. He also means that the norms in accord with which that power must be exercised must be thought of as determined by citizens, conceived of as free, equal, and fairly situated. In their public life and for political purposes, citizens must be able to view themselves as the source of those norms.

Once we see that Rawls accepts the strong interpretation of (6), it is clear why he would also accept (33). For (33) says that when citizens appeal to political principles drawn from a conception which does not stand free of comprehensive doctrine, they propose to exercise power in a way not justifiable to each as a coholder of society's final power. And once we see why he accepts (33), it is clear why he also accepts (34) and thinks that citizens as such have the associated interests and expectations. A citizen unwilling to show that her political principles are independent of comprehensive doctrine is also unwilling publicly to treat herself and others as the source of those principles. The claim that (34) lays down a condition of the most appropriate forms of trust and respect thus depends upon the claim that American citizens are appropriately thought of as exercising final political power in the strong sense of "final" that Rawls uses in (6). If they are, then they have a role-specific interest in being treated by one another as free and equal coholders of their society's final political power in this sense. They should try to cultivate the expectation that they will be so treated if they do not have it already. And they should be or should strive to become the kind of citizens whose respect for and trust in one another depend upon that expectation's being satisfied.

This is, I suspect, quite a burdensome demand to place on American citizens. Many, I would conjecture, think that they are *not* coholders of society's final power as Rawls understands it. Coming to believe that they are, and that they should treat one another as such, would require significant changes in their beliefs and structure of motives. Philosophical considerations alone do not decide whether such changes would be justified. However attractive political autonomy may be, it is necessary to look at the costs to democracy of making the changes that political autonomy demands. The accounting is, in part, an empirical matter. The costs and benefits can be balanced accurately only if we look at what political and cultural institutions shape American political psychology, and at what costs and benefits those institutions confer on American politics.

Membership in religious secondary associations and churches accounts for the fact that many Americans think themselves subject to principles of justice of which they are not the authors. It also accounts for why so many citizens argue about fundamental matters of justice in religious terms, using just the arguments that Rawls thinks must be made good by appeal to public reason. I have argued elsewhere that churches do much to make American political processes as democratic as they are. Their contributions, I have argued, should be recognized by proponents of a variety of democratic theories, from the pluralistic to the deliberative.[54] This is especially true of black churches, which provide virtually the only institutional counterweight to the very sources of political inequality that African-American voters and politicians so often use religious arguments to combat. It is true as well of churches that minister to and speak on behalf of the poor. I think it unlikely that American churches and religious organizations will soon teach their members to regard themselves and their fellow citizens as the coauthors of norms in accord with which political power must be exercised in fundamental cases. The conception of citizenship according to which they are can therefore take hold only if churches, religious organizations and religious leaders play far less prominent roles in the political lives of their congregants than they now do. The costs to American democracy of their doing so would, I believe, be too high to pay. Thus the strong interpretation of (6) expresses a conception of citizenship that is inappropriate for the contemporary United States, given the role that churches play in democratizing American politics. The conclusion Rawls reaches in the second stage of the argument—that (36) expresses a role-specific duty binding on American citizens—depends upon the appropriateness of that conception. I conclude that (36) does not express such a duty.[55]

Conclusion

When I discussed the first stage of Rawls's argument, I endorsed the claim that citizens must be willing, as a matter of role-specific duty, to show how their positions can be supported by a reasonable balance of political values. Since this is implied by (26) and since (26) depends upon (6), why doesn't my rejection of (6) undermine this conclusion as well? The answer is that I have not rejected (6) *simpliciter*. Nor have I categorically rejected a strong interpretation of it, which may be a useful way to think of citizens for some purposes. I have claimed only that a strong interpretation of (6) is incompatible with a conception of citizenship that is appropriate for determining citizens' role-specific duties with respect to public political argument. The claim about those duties that I endorsed does not depend upon the strong interpretation.

Someone might object that the conception of citizenship implicit in my endorsement of this claim is no more appropriate for the contemporary United States than is Rawls's. For if citizens are to be capable of defending their positions by appeal to a balance of political values, they will have to be able to distinguish political values from other values and must have some sense of how to balance them. There are religious traditions that harbor deep suspicions about even rudimentary philosophical inquiry and education needed to draw this distinction and deploy it when necessary. There are fundamentalisms that reject the modernist differentiation of life and deny that the political is a distinct sphere of activity in which nontheological moral values are realized. The appropriate conception of citizenship for a society in which these religious strains are represented must accommodate them. My response is merely to assert that I have relied on a minimal conception of citizenship. Citizenship is by nature a political relation among individuals and between individuals and the state. When citizens of a democracy consider their common business as such, they ought not do so without reference to the requirements of equality and of the political common good of their society. To deny this is not to deny my claims about how citizenship is appropriately conceived. It is instead to deny that the notion of citizenship is relevant to the question of how political argument should proceed.

I have suggested that citizens may publicly appeal to political principles dependent upon comprehensive doctrine without providing the further argument (36) would ask of them. It does not follow, of course, that I favor every or even most policies that those principles are used to support. I have little sympathy for the political agenda of either intellectual neoconservatives or the American religious right. But it is very important to distinguish those who violate the obligations of citizenship from those with whose politics we vehemently disagree. Charging that others violated their duties by flouting the guidelines of public reason will only exacerbate the incivility that motivated the search for those guidelines in the first place.

Finally, what of Rawls's conception of citizenship, resting as it does on the strong interpretation of (6)? Rawls refers to that conception as an ideal, yet ideals cannot ground obligations. I therefore argue that he should not be read as putting forward an ideal. Instead he should be read as offering a specification of the role of citizenship that he thinks carries with it role-specific duties with respect to public political argument. I have suggested, however, that that specification is not appropriate and that it cannot ground duties binding on us. This does not imply that we should reject or neglect the Rawlsian conception of citizenship. We can follow Rawls in taking it as an ideal, but reject the claim that it imposes a duty. As an ideal, it can help us to locate various sources of incivility in our political life. By reflecting on it, we can come to appreciate the value of self-restraint in political argument and to recognize ways in which our own political behavior could be more civil. It can make vivid and attractive one form that relationship might take and one set of values it might realize. It does not, however, vivify a form citizenship must take or a form of civility we are obliged to pursue.

Notes

1. John Rawls "The Idea of Public Reason Revisited," *The University of Chicago Law Review,* 64 (1997), p. 765.
2. A well-ordered society is one in which everyone accepts and knows that everyone else accepts the same principles of justice, and the basic structure satisfies and is generally known to satisfy those principles. The deep disagreements in American politics about how to balance liberty and equality, which motivate justice as fairness, are evidence that American society is not well ordered at all. To cite just two reasons why I assume it is not well ordered by Rawls's conception

of justice, the political liberties lack fair value and the difference principle is not satisfied.

3. See John Rawls, *Political Liberalism* (New York: Columbia University Press, 1996), p. 243 n. 32, the explanation of this on pp. lv–lvii, notes 31–33; see also "Public Reason Revisited," pp. 798–99, notes 80–83. All references to *Political Liberalism* below are to the paperback edition.

4. Rawls, *Political Liberalism*, pp. 248ff.

5. Ibid., p. lii.

6. Rawls, "Public Reason Revisited," p. 767.

7. Ibid.

8. Rawls, *Political Liberalism*, p. 215.

9. It might seem unnecessarily convoluted to argue that citizens must justify their votes to one another on certain grounds because this would encourage candidates to appeal for votes on those grounds. Why not employ the more economical argument that citizens must be able to justify their votes to one another because they exercise power over one another by voting? In fact, Rawls does offer the simpler argument in *Political Liberalism*, pp. 217–20. I offer the more complicated one here to accommodate Rawls's remark in "Public Reason Revisited" that citizens honor the idea of public reason by holding candidates and government officials to it.

10. For the notion of deliberative democracy, see Joshua Cohen, Deliberation and Democratic Legitimacy, in *The Good Polity*, ed. Alan Hamlin and Philip Pettit, Oxford: Basil Blackwell, 1991, pp. 17–34.

11. Rawls, "Public Reason Revisited," pp. 771ff.

12. Rawls, *Political Liberalism*, p. 215.

13. Rawls, "Public Reason Revisited," p. 768 n.10.

14. For Martin Luther King, Jr. see Rawls, *Political Liberalism*, pp. 250ff.; for Cardinal Bernardin, see "Public Reason Revisited," p. 798 n.82.

15. On Sunday, May 24, 1998, John Cardinal O'Connor of New York delivered a homily critical of a domestic partnership act under consideration by the New York City Council. Reporting on the homily, *The New York Times* wrote, "Cardinal O'Connor . . . is perhaps the only person in New York with a platform to rival that of the mayor." The story went on to say of the Cardinal: "[H]e seems to

revel in the role: his plan to discuss the domestic partnership bill had been announced. The cathedral has a platform for television news cameras with jacks for them to plug into the sound system, and the Cardinal's staff distributed the seven-page text of his homily—with the most newsworthy passages in bold type." (*The New York Times*, May 25, 1998, pp. A1 and B5).

A publicly announced homily in a church with facilities to accommodate the media, delivered by a cleric of Cardinal O'Connor's visibility, on a public matter (albeit not a constitutional essential), seems to me to take place in the public forum. More generally, it seems to me that a cleric of influence can, on occasion, make the church pulpit a public forum, though of course it is not always one.

16. Rawls, "Public Reason Revisited," pp. 769–70.

17. Rawls, *Political Liberalism*, p. 68; on p. 139 he says that "the basic framework of social life [is] the very groundwork of our existence."

18. Ibid., p. 214.

19. Ibid., p. 61.

20. This is not to say that democratic theory need be silent about the ways parental, pedagogical and communal power are exercised over children. It is merely to say that where democratic theory has implications, they do not follow from the claim that authority to exercise the power in question is derived from the authority of those over whom it is exercised.

21. Rawls, "Public Reason Revisited," p. 766 (emphasis added).

22. I use the rather cumbersome phrase "evince their will" for two reasons. One is that it is a matter of debate whether votes and contributions to public deliberation are best understood as expressions of opinion, of preference or of proposed collective aims. (See David Estlund, "Democracy Without Preference," *The Philosophical Review*, 94 (1990), 397–423; also Henry S. Richardson, "Democratic Intentions," *Deliberative Democracy: Essays on Reason and Politics,* ed. James Bohman and William Rehg. Cambridge, Mass: MIT Press, 1997, pp. 349–82.) My phrase is neutral on this complicated matter. The second is that the word "evince" captures the fact that citizens' discourse may be intended to express their will or may reasonably be taken by others to express it, or both.

23. Rawls, *Political Liberalism*, p. 217.

24. Ibid.
25. Ibid., p. 243.
26. Ibid., p. 218.
27. This would not follow even if each of us were required to do what is within our power to make our society well ordered, since it is not clear that our society would be more effectively made that way by honoring the guidelines or by violating them. The elaborate provisions that Rawls's account of public reason originally included, to deal with just this question, are among the parts of the original view he later disavowed as unnecessary. See *Political Liberalism*, p. lii.
28. Rawls, *Political Liberalism*, p. 218.
29. Ibid., p. 217.
30. I am very grateful to Nick Wolterstorff for invaluable conversations about the matters covered in this and the next three paragraphs.
31. Cf. John Rawls, *A Theory of Justice*. Cambridge, Mass.: Harvard University Press, 1971, p. 477: "Best of all, a theory should present a description of an ideally just state of affairs, a conception of a well ordered society such that the aspiration to realize this state of affairs, and to maintain it in being, answers to our good and is continuous with our natural sentiments. A perfectly just society should be part of an ideal that rational human beings could desire more than anything else once they had full knowledge and experience of what it was."
32. For the notion of a conception-dependent desire, see Rawls, *Political Liberalism*, pp. 82ff.
33. I exempt Japan, where I gather there are relatively few such associations. (I am grateful to a lecture by Seymour Martin Lipset for this point.)
34. Rawls, "Public Reason Revisited," p. 776.
35. Cf. Iris Marion Young, "Difference as a Resource for Democratic Communication," in Bohman and Rehg, *Deliberative Democracy*, pp. 383–406.
36. Nicholas Wolterstorff, "Why We Should Reject What Liberalism Tells Us about Speaking and Acting in Public for Religious Reasons," in *Religion and Contemporoary Liberalism*, ed. Paul J. Weithman. Notre Dame, Ind.: University of Notre Dame Press, 1997, pp. 162–81.
37. Rawls, "Public Reason Revisited," p. 776.

38. See John Finnis, "On the Practical Meaning of Secularism," *Notre Dame Law Review*, 73 (1998), 491–93; also David Hollenbach "Politically Active Churches: Some Empirical Prolegomena to a Normative Approach," in Weithman, *Religion and Contemporary Liberalism*, pp. 291–306.

39. This objection is pressed forcefully by Michael R. DePaul in "Liberal Exclusions and Foundationalism," *Ethical Theory and Moral Practice*, 1 (1998), pp. 118–19 n. 30.

40. Cf. John Locke, *The Second Treatise on Civil Government*, in Locke, *Two Treatises of Goverment*. Cambridge, UK: Cambridge University Press, 1988, ed. Peter Laslett, paragraph 2: "To this purpose, I think it may not be amiss to set down what I take to be Political Power. That the Power of a *Magistrate* over a Subject, may be distinguished from that of a *Father* over his Children, a *Master* over his Servant, a *Husband* over his Wife, and a *Lord* over his Slave. All which distinct Powers happening sometimes together in the same Man, if he be considered under these different Relations, it may help us to distinguish these Powers from one another, and shew the difference betwixt a Ruler of a Common-wealth, a Father of a Family, and a Captain of a Galley."

41. Rawls, "Public Reason Revisited," p. 766 (emphasis added).

42. Ibid., p. 776.

43. Ibid.

44. Ibid.

45. To illustrate the difference, I do not believe that Cardinal O'Connor's homily, referred to in n. 15 above, is cast in the form of public reason. *The New York Times* reported: "Cardinal O'Connor . . . acknowledged that the church 'has no right to impose specifically Catholic teaching on others,' and said it had no desire to do so. Instead, he couched his criticism in nonsectarian terms that seemed intended to resonate beyond the Gothic cathedral on Fifth Avenue." It also quoted him as saying, "It is imperative, in my judgment, that no law be passed contrary to the natural moral law and Western tradition by virtually legislating that 'marriage does not matter.'" The Cardinal's appeal to natural law as the source of his nonsectarian political premises, and the absence of any acknowledgment that those premises could be supported by

a freestanding political conception, is what seems to violate the second condition.

46. Here I gloss over an important complication. We need not accept the supposition that there are no reasons for prohibiting assisted suicide which do not ultimately depend upon comprehensive doctrine. We need only suppose that the agent thinks there are no other grounds. Even if she is wrong to think this, I believe Rawls would still say that she violates a role-specific duty in arguing as she does because she evinces her willingness to coerce others on the basis of her comprehensive doctrine. In fact, I think the agent in my example is wrong and that there are compelling reasons for prohibiting physician-assisted suicide which do not depend on comprehensive doctrine. See my "Of Assisted Suicide and 'The Philosophers' Brief'," *Ethics*, 109 (1999), 548–78.

47. Rawls, *Political Liberalism*, p. 37.

48. For a sophisticated attempt to find a basis of agreement in King's views, see Joshua Cohen, "The Arc of the Moral Universe," *Philosophy and Public Affairs*, 26 (1997), 91–134, esp. pp. 133–34. See also Taylor Branch, "An Uneasy Holiday," where he interprets King as thinking that "religion and democratic politics are united in their purest essences and yearning." ("An Uneasy Holiday" originally appeared in *The New Republic* on February 3, 1986. It is reprinted in *The New Republic Reader,* ed. Dorothy Wickenden [New York: Basic Books, 1994] pp. 419–28; the quoted passage occurs on p. 426.)

49. In his review of Taylor Branch, *Pillar of Fire: America in the King Years, 1963–65,* New York: Simon and Schuster, 1997, Alan Wolfe wrote: "Against all these forces, Martin Luther King Jr. managed to build upon America's religious and moral foundations to uphold the dignity of the individual. . . . [H]e said of civil rights demonstrators: 'The patter of their feet as they walked through the Jim Crow barriers in the great stride toward freedom is the thunder of the marching men of Joshua. And the world rocks beneath their tread. My people, my people, listen, listen, the battle is in our hands.' In the aftermath of the Birmingham bombing, King spoke not of retribution but of redemption . . . Words like this are rarely heard in American politics these days, because so few have the moral stature

to utter them." (*The New York Times Book Review,* January 18, 1998, p. 13.)

50. Abraham Joshua Heschel, *Moral Grandeur and Spiritual Audacity,* ed. Susannah Heschel, New York: Farrar, Straus, Giroux, 1996, p. vii.

51. After marching in Selma with Martin Luther King, Heschel wrote in his diary: "I felt again what I have been thinking about for years—that Jewish religious institutions have again missed a great opportunity, namely, to interpret a civil-rights movement in terms of Judaism. The vast number of Jews participating actively in it are totally unaware of what the movement means in terms of the prophetic traditions." (Ibid., pp. xxiii–xxiv.)

I am, of course, only asking what our reactions would be if Heschel would have refused to justify his conclusions by appeal to public reason. I do not know that he would have refused.

52. See the questions raised in Rawls, "Public Reason Revisited," p. 776.

53. Rawls, *Political Liberalism,* p. 97.

54. See ch. 1 and 3 of Weithman, forthcoming, on file with author.

55. Though I cannot pursue the matter here, I would argue that there are non-Rawlsian forms of trust, respect, and civic friendship that are available in a society in which citizens settle fundamental questions by appeal to political values but do not honor (36).

Patrick Neal

Political Liberalism, Public Reason, and the Citizen of Faith

Introduction

The idea of public reason is arguably the most novel and interesting aspect of John Rawls's account of political liberalism. Certainly it has proved to be one of the most controversial aspects of his post-*A Theory of Justice* writings. One area of political thinking that has proved highly stimulating is that concerned with the relation between religion and politics, especially religion and liberal politics. Recently, Rawls has "revisited" the idea of public reason, expanding, clarifying, and in one significant case changing the ideas that were originally articulated in the chapter of *Political Liberalism* devoted to the subject.[1] In this essay I examine Rawls's ideas of political liberalism and public reason as they relate to religion, especially in the form personified by the representative character Rawls refers to as the "citizen of faith."

Much of the reaction by religious thinkers to Rawls's idea of public reason and the alleged requirements it imposes upon citizens in a constitutional democracy has been critical, if not hostile. Rawls is generally portrayed, along with Bruce Ackerman and

Ronald Dworkin, as supporting the idea that religious discourse has no proper place in the public realm of a liberal democracy. This simple description of his position is not entirely inaccurate, but it is inaccurate in some ways. Rawls's views on the relation between religion and liberal public reason are highly complex, and also quite qualified and limited in terms of the nature of the restrictions they would impose upon religious believers. Paul Weithman, in his reading of Rawls's ideas as the primary exemplar of the "liberalism of reasoned respect," has usefully pointed out just how limited these restrictions are, if one imagines them as actual practical proposals.[2]

However, I don't think the critical reaction to Rawls from religious thinkers derives in any serious sense from the hypothetical burden that his strictures might place upon them. Rather, I think it derives primarily from the belief that the structure of Rawlsian liberalism treats religious believers unfairly, and that it does this because it misunderstands what "religion" or the "religious perspective" is. Thus, from this critical perspective, it doesn't much matter how heavy the burden of Rawlsian public reason would actually be if one had to bear it in an actual regime. Indeed, I suppose that many religious citizens would simply ignore the requirements of what Rawls calls the "duty of civility" to participate in liberal public reason, since they would think it an unjustified demand in the first place.[3] In any case, the charge that Rawls's account of liberalism misunderstands the perspective of the religious citizen and consequently treats it unfairly is one that is important to consider, regardless of whether the duty of civility imposes requirements that are light and inconsequential or not.

It is this charge I am concerned with in this essay. I believe that there is a specific sense in which the charge is justified, and it is that sense that I hope to demonstrate through an analysis of certain aspects of Rawls's texts. So, in spite of the fact that there are, in my view, features of Rawls's "revisitation" of public reason which make the doctrine somewhat less objectionable (in the sense of "lighter to bear") from the point of view of a "citizen of faith," there remains an aspect of the doctrine which must of necessity render it unacceptable to such a citizen, or at least to very many of them. Moreover, the rejection of the (alleged) duty to liberal public reason upon the basis of this feature seems to me entirely reasonable, and I hope to show why it is that Rawls, or a defender of Rawlsian liberalism, would be wrong to think otherwise.

I shall call the feature that renders the requirement of public reason, as Rawls understands it, objectionable to the citizen of faith, the "issue of authority." I shall further call the feature of Rawls's account that leads it to misunderstand (in my view) the citizen of faith's reasonable rejection of public reason arising out of the issue of authority, the "misdescription of the challenge." My claim is that Rawls's account of liberal justice and public reason provides a distorted description of the religious challenge to public reason, and that this distortion is the source of the mistaken view that it would be unreasonable to reject what Rawls calls the "duty of civility," a key component of which is to participate in public reason (as Rawls understands it) when making decisions about basic justice and constitutional essentials.

The Issue of Authority and the Misdescription of the Challenge to Political Liberalism

The basic idea I have in mind in referring to the "issue of authority" is simple. I understand a citizen of faith to be one who owes ultimate allegiance to God, and who believes that it is incumbent upon him to live according to the will of God.[4] Of course, this apparently simple formulation raises a host of vexing questions. In a sense, these questions (Who is God? Is God knowable? In what senses? By what methods? What is the will of God? How can it be known? and so forth) are the heart of religion as a human practice, for one way of thinking about religious activity is as the enterprise by which such questions are addressed and lived by collectivities of human beings. Such activity is endlessly complex and varied. Yet in contrast to that, it seems to me simple and clear that for many citizens of faith, the general question of what constitutes the final authority for life is a very easily answered one: God.

Moreover, for at least many Christian citizens of faith, the importance of *acknowledging* this authority and the danger of the corresponding *temptation* to deny it are absolutely central to their self-understanding. The tension between the ways of man and the ways of God, and more particularly between the claims of Caesar and the claims of Christ, are central themes in Christian narrative. Christian self-consciousness is at least partly structured around such dualistic tensions. This consciousness sets the context within which all questions of politics arise for the Christian citizen of faith.

It is in light of these considerations that we might look at the issue of the relation between political liberalism and (Christian) citizens of faith. In "The Idea of Public Reason Revisited," Rawls frames the issue of the relation between political liberalism and religion in the form of a very provocatively phrased question. He asks: "How is it possible for citizens of faith to be wholehearted members of a democratic society who endorse society's intrinsic political ideals and values and do not simply acquiesce in the balance of political and social forces?"[5] Now from the point of view of a citizen of faith, the most striking feature of this question is the use of the phrase "wholehearted." Put simply, that phrase more or less settles the issue immediately. It is not possible (except at the cost of betrayal) for a Christian to be a "wholehearted" member of *any* society, Rawlsian, liberal, democratic, or other, with the exception of that City about which glorious things are spoken. I submit that no thoughtful Christian ought to profess "wholehearted" allegiance to any political regime, or any set of principles specifying a political regime.[6]

Of course, this is to put a great deal of weight on the phrase "wholehearted." The meaning of that phrase is unspecified in Rawls's account, and indeed the term may have been used by him in a more or less loose and casual sense, perhaps employed more for rhetorical effect than for cognitive content.[7] The term is not repeated after the single use cited above. One can thus imagine Rawls responding to my point along the following lines: "Oh, you're reading entirely too much into that phrase. I'm not asking you to sell your soul, after all. The question is whether you can affirm the principles of political justice outlined in political liberalism in a more than merely pragmatic way. My concern is that there be an overlapping consensus of support for the political conception of justice, and not simply a *modus vivendi*. The issue, then, is whether a citizen of faith's comprehensive religious view is such that it can affirm as a matter of right, and not simply expediency, a commitment to abide by the liberal principles of political justice. So let's interpret the phrase 'wholehearted' to mean simply 'more than expedient agreement,' where it is further understood that such agreement does not necessarily mean that the political values will or even should necessarily take priority over the terms of one's comprehensive view."

Let's call this the "weak" reading of the requirement that allegiance to political liberalism be "wholehearted." A "strong" reading would be one that took the requirement to mean that the principles of political liberalism should take priority over provisions of one's comprehensive moral or religious view in cases of conflict. I take it as obvious that many citizens of faith could not accept the strong reading of the condition, and I believe such citizens would be entirely reasonable in rejecting it. Indeed, it seems to me that it would be unreasonable, not to say morally irresponsible, to accept it.

Now let us consider Rawls' understanding of the relation between political liberalism and comprehensive views in light of these two possible readings. In "The Idea of Public Reason Revisited," Rawls gives two cases where political stability around liberal principles is achieved, but not "for the right reasons."[8] The first is the case of "Catholics and Protestants in the sixteenth and seventeenth centuries when the principle of toleration was honored only as a *modus vivendi*. This meant that should either party fully gain its way it would impose its own religious doctrine as the sole admissible faith."[9] In commenting upon this case, Rawls refers not to the failure of the parties to manifest "wholehearted" commitment to liberal principles, but rather to their failure to evidence "a firm allegiance" to them. Note that the "firmness" of the allegiance is for Rawls a function not of the actual degree to which the parties uphold the agreement, but rather to the underlying rationale for upholding the agreement. A party under suspicion for failing to meet this test will find it difficult to prove its good will, since no amount of actual commitment and behavior will be sufficient to display the necessary rationale. One might consider in this respect the long-standing attitude regarding Catholics and Jews in a predominantly Protestant American culture, which held that whatever their actual behavior, one could never be sure of the ultimate basis of their commitment to the regime.

The second case is that of "a democratic society where citizens accept as political (moral) principles the substantive constitutional clauses that ensure religious, political, and civil liberties, when their allegiance to these constitutional principles is so limited that none is willing to see his or her religious or nonreligious doctrine losing ground in influence and numbers, and such citizens are prepared to resist and disobey laws that they think undermine their positions."[10] Commenting on this case, Rawls says that "here again, democracy is accepted conditionally and not for the right reasons."[11]

Now each of these cases has the form of relating instances that fail the test of "affirmation for the right reasons," but neither case specifies what would be necessary to pass the test. The difference is important from the point of view of the citizen of faith. The question from this point of view is whether there is any "space" between the two instances of failing the test and the instance of passing it by expressing "firm allegiance" through "wholehearted commitment" in the strong sense. I think that from the point of view of the citizen of faith there are other possibilities than these, and indeed that the citizen of faith will claim to occupy one of them.

Consider that as Rawls portrays the situation, the threat to "stability for the right reasons" is constituted by the threat of self-interested action. In each of the two examples, a sufficiently firm commitment to liberal principles of political justice is withheld for what essentially amount to considerations of advancing one's, or one's group's, personal interests. Rawls himself acknowledges this description in remarking that "what these examples have in common is that society is divided into separate groups, each of which has its own fundamental interest distinct from and opposed to the interests of the other groups and for which it is prepared to resist or to violate legitimate democratic law."[12] Placed in opposition to such selfish behavior is the commitment to political liberalism "for the right reasons," that is, a willingness to assent to those principles even in cases where there is a conflict with the dictates of one's comprehensive view.

But what this excludes from consideration is the case where one refuses wholehearted assent to the terms of political liberalism for moral reasons, rather than for reasons of self-interest. In effect, Rawls' description of the situation leaves no conceptual room for this possibility. This has the consequence of distorting the nature of at least some dissent from the principles of political liberalism, including dissent arising from the claims of faith upon citizens of faith. To put it simply, it is wrong to suppose that there can be no morally principled dissent from wholehearted allegiance to the principles of political liberalism. Upon this supposition, people who dissent upon the grounds of moral principle are wrongly portrayed as if they were simply selfish people who place their own personal interest (or their group's interest) above the demands of justice and the common good. But this is not necessarily so. Some dissenters will object not because they *ignore* such demands, but rather because they do not agree with Rawls's considered opinion that those demands are fulfilled by the particular doctrine of political liberalism. In short, they will object because they think Rawls is *wrong*, not because they are selfish. Now of course, it is possible that they will, from an objective point of view, be wrong about this. But it is possible that Rawls is wrong too. Assuming honest reflection and good faith on the part of both, we are left with a disagreement about how best to specify the demands of justice. That is quite a different thing from a disagreement between those who support justice and those who are selfish scoundrels.

The difference can be seen vividly when one considers Rawls's comments on religious dissent in "The Idea of Public Reason Revisited." He remarks that "while no one is expected to put his or her religious or nonreligious doctrine in danger, we must give up forever the hope of changing the constitution so as to establish our religion's hegemony, or of qualifying our obligations so as to ensure its influence and success."[13] I am not sure what the first part of this passage means, but the relevant feature for present purposes is the way in which dissent is imagined to arise from strategic considerations of self-interest. But surely not all dissent from political liberalism is nothing more than this. Suppose, for example, that a qualified right to abortion as a basic constitutional right is a consequence of political liberalism, a view that Rawls holds. Consider now those who disagree that abortion is just, and who, at least partly as a consequence of this belief, reject political liberalism (because they agree with Rawls that, analytically, a right to abortion is a consequence of the principles of political liberalism). To describe such persons as trying to establish the "hegemony" of their religion in the face of the demands of justice, or to ensure their religion's "influence and success" against the demands of justice, is simply wrong. They, or at least some of them, are rejecting political liberalism *in the name of* justice, not *in spite of* it.

There are two levels at which it is a distortion to describe the challenger's rejection of political liberalism as an act of self-interest. First, the challenger may be seen as claiming to act in the name of the same value, viz. justice, as does the political liberal. "Justice," understood generally, is the name of that at which political activity is to be aimed. I take this as an analytical truism, at least for any normative theory of politics. But it doesn't tell us what "justice" requires of us, and a conscientious political actor will have to hold some more specific idea of justice (some interpretation of the general idea) in order to act in accord with a duty to act justly. Rawls's theory of "justice as fairness" is an example of such a specification. But there are numerous other specifications, many of them, like "justice as fairness," articulated and defended and reflected upon by intelligent and conscientious men and women of good will and sense. It may be that justice as fairness (or some other view) is the best specification of the general idea of justice; but we have no way of knowing that, or, at least, we have no way of demonstrating it such that all reasonable people can be made to agree. Reasonable people of good will disagree about what justice requires of us.[14] At this level, then, dissenters from political liberalism will be misdescribed as selfish whenever they in fact dissent, because they believe, upon the basis of reflection, that political liberalism is not the best specification of the value of justice.

Let's consider a second level at which it can be distorting to treat dissent as a matter of self-interest. At this level, we grant, for the sake of argument, the idea that political liberalism is in fact the best and truest specification of the idea of justice, such that anyone who recognizes a duty to justice ought to affirm wholeheartedly the principles of political liberalism. Even on this counterfactual assumption, it still seems to me it would be wrong to describe dissenters as if they were best understood as selfish pursuers of their own interests. Insofar as they seek justice but fail to correctly see that it entails political liberalism and thus continue to dissent, they are making a mistake, not pursuing an interest.

One of the curious things about Rawls's treatment of dissent here is that he himself, in other contexts, gives very strong voice to considerations and ideas that would seem to lead one to recognize the points I have been making above. Thus, in regard to the first level above, Rawls has stressed the senses in which the exercise of human powers under conditions of freedom will lead to a plurality of reasonable, but different and incompatible, conceptions of the good. He has insisted that this pluralism not be understood as "disaster but rather as the natural outcome of the activities of human reason under enduring free institutions. To see reasonable pluralism as a disaster is to see the exercise of reason under the conditions of freedom itself as a disaster."[15] I agree with Rawls's view in this respect, but not with the limitation of its relevance to views of the good only. As per above, I see no reason not to acknowledge reasonable disagreement about justice.

In regard to the second level above, where we assume for the sake of argument that political liberalism is objectively the correct specification of justice, Rawls has again articulated reasons that would seem to tell in favor of recognizing that dissent from affirmation of political liberalism is (at least sometimes) rooted in conscientious but mistaken reasoning (in the name of justice and the common good) rather than in selfishness. I refer here to his notion of the "burdens of judgment."[16] The burdens of judgment are those factors that explain how it is that reasonable people who employ their powers of reflection nevertheless fail to agree. Moreover, the factors are such that they are "fully compatible with" and "do not impugn the reasonableness" of those who disagree, as opposed to factors (like irrationality, stupidity, self-deceit) that do impugn their practitioners. Rawls's account of the burdens of judgment is subtle and sensitive to the many ways in which moral reasoning is unable to generate anything resembling simple, clear and precise "answers" to questions about the moral life. Nevertheless, when Rawls imagines religious dissent from political liberalism in the passages considered above, consideration of the burdens of judgment and the naturalness of pluralism arising from the free exercise of human reason seem to recede from the portrayal of the situation, to be replaced with portraits of people who are either lying in wait to break a *modus vivendi* or, at best, following the principles of political liberalism only up to the point at which the "influence and success" of "their religion" is ensured.

This creates an ambiguous picture with respect to the citizen of faith. Recall that on the weak reading, affirmation for the right reasons would occur if one did not affirm political liberalism simply for reasons of prudent self-interest. The weak interpretation operates by specifying what counts as a *violation* of the test of right reasons, but without specifying what counts as fulfillment of it. The two cases from Rawls's text considered above are clear violations of the weak interpretation of the test. The "strong" interpretation would need to lay down explicit criteria of what is necessary to pass the test, where "explicit" means a statement of positive expectations. No such statement is given on the weak interpretation, for it defines the criteria negatively, i.e., as "not for reasons of prudent self-interest." Such a negative formulation leaves open the issue of exactly what sorts of nonprudential reasons would qualify as sufficient to pass the test. The "strong" interpretation of the idea of affirmation for the right reasons would be one which spoke directly to this question.

Rawls's text does not clarify this ambiguity. He gives explicit cases of examples exemplifying failure to meet the test, but no explicit examples of success. The extent of his specification of the positive criteria necessary to constitute a "strong" interpretation of the test is the employment of a series of terms, the meaning of which is difficult to pin down beyond the sense that they all are meant to denote "something other than prudential self-interest." The terms include "wholehearted," "endorsement," and "firm allegiance."

Now this ambiguity may seem a trivial one, but I suspect that is true only if one is examining the matter from the perspective of the Rawlsian liberal rather than from that of the citizen of faith. The Rawlsian liberal sees two fundamental possibilities: wholehearted, firm allegiance to the principles of political liberalism, or a refusal of such, rooted in self-interest (or the interests of one's group). It is against this dichotomous background that religious dissent from the principles of political liberalism comes to be colored as mere selfishness. But from the perspective of the citizen of faith, there is another, third, possibility. This would be a qualified and hedged commitment to the regime based on the principles of political liberalism, where the hedge derived not from self-interest, but rather from the view that political principles and activities must always be checked against the standard of moral truth, a standard that will be ultimately theological for the citizen of faith. This is, from the perspective of the citizen of faith, a form of commitment that is wrongly characterized if it is reduced to nothing more than prudent self-interest. On the other hand, it is a form of commitment that may fail to satisfy the Rawlsian notions of "wholehearted" commitment and "firm" allegiance. That it so fails need not, of course, be a source of concern to the citizen of faith, anymore than she need be concerned to discover that her conscientious judgments in the name of justice fail to agree with anyone else's. It may well be a matter of concern to her, however, that (assuming she is living under a regime governed by the principles of political liberalism) her standing as an actor is being systematically misdescribed by the perspective of political liberalism. What she understands and describes as a disagreement between her and the political liberal about justice is redescribed by the political liberal as a case of someone avoiding justice in pursuit of self-interest.

It is just this difference that I think informs much of the criticism of Rawls advanced by thinkers writing from a religious perspective, that is, by actual citizens of faith. The point will be especially vivid if we leave aside for the moment religious critics of Rawls who would be characterized as "conservative" in conventional political or theological senses, and concentrate on religious critics who would conventionally be understood as "liberal" in a political and theological sense. At first glance it might seem difficult to understand why there should be any serious disagreement at all between Rawls's political liberalism and the viewpoint of citizens who are religious liberals. Certainly it is Rawls's intention to avoid such disagreement, for he hopes to attract such believers into the overlapping consensus of support for political liberalism. He says that religious comprehensive views (excepting what he refers to as "fundamentalist views") can be reasonable on his account, and he maintains that (some) religious comprehensive views can be understood as passing the test of providing the necessary principled consent to political liberalism.[17] He goes out of his way to stress that political liberalism is not to be confused with, and indeed that it rejects, "enlightenment liberalism, which historically attacked orthodox Christianity."[18] Nevertheless, I am not sure he is fully aware of the difficulty for the citizen of faith created by his insistence on affirmation of political liberalism for the right reasons. Here is where the "issue of authority" becomes crucial in understanding the relation between the citizen of faith and political liberalism.

The citizen of faith who is politically liberal in the everyday sense of that term may very well reach agreement on any number of substantive political and policy issues with the Rawlsian liberal. Indeed, in order to help clarify ideas, let's imagine our liberal citizen of faith agreeing with every position the Rawlsian liberal takes on substantive issues of policy. Still, the citizen of faith cannot accept the strong reading of the idea that her commitment to political liberalism must be wholehearted and firm. This reading would insist that the principles of justice characteristic of political liberalism should take priority over provisions of one's comprehensive moral or religious view in cases of conflict. The citizen of faith could not grant this much authority to political liberalism without denying the ultimate authority of God. Now note that this does *not* mean that the citizen of faith cannot commit herself to some of the values that Rawls characteristically describes as part and parcel of political liberalism. She may well believe that liberty of conscience and equality of citizenship are fundamental aspects of a just political regime, and that she is bound to support such principles in practice. Insofar as she is committed to these practices, it will be because the conception of political justice yielded up by her comprehensive religious beliefs specifies them as just. It may seem that there is no tension here between her and the Rawlsian liberal, and indeed there is not in regard to the practices of liberty of conscience and equality of citizenship. The rub comes over the issue of authority, when the citizen of faith is asked to further agree to the idea that she will eschew reliance on her comprehensive beliefs, and instead rely only on political reasons drawn from liberal public reason, when making political judgments (at least on "constitutional essentials and matters of basic justice"). This request the citizen of faith must deny. Not because she is selfish, nor because she hopes to destroy liberty of conscience and equal citizenship in favor of the triumph of her own religion (indeed, she may be dismayed to hear that this conflict is presupposed in the description of the fear given by Rawls), but rather because the principles of political liberalism are not ultimately authoritative for her, and must always be checked against the standard of truth, a standard that she refuses to bracket from questions of basic justice and constitutional essentials. No matter how much she may agree with the particular provisions of political liberalism, this agreement will be based upon her ultimate religious commitments, and understood by her as derivative from and secondary to them.

It may be easier to see the point if we consider how the same issue comes up in respect to another aspect of Rawls's theory of justice. Consider, for illustration, the concept of the original position as originally developed in *A Theory of Justice*. The principles of justice were to be understood as those chosen from the point of view modeled on the idea of the original position, a position wherein the agents would be deprived of information that was "irrelevant from the standpoint of justice."[19] For our present purpose, the noteworthy feature is that Rawls treated knowledge of a conception of the good as among the things excluded. It was then lumped into the same functional category as knowledge of one's social and economic status. The concern, from the point of view of contractarianism, is that knowledge of matters falling into this category could be exploited by the agent in ways that could subvert justice in service of the agent's interests. Rawls claimed that "[i]t also seems widely agreed that it should be impossible to tailor principles to the circumstances of one's own case."[20] Thus insisting upon reasoning about political justice in light of one's understanding of the good comes to be treated as similar to the activity of insisting that principles of political order be tailored to insure that one's interests are treated as superior to those of others. But this simply makes a travesty of the understanding of the relation between justice and the good maintained by those who disagree with the Rawlsian position that places the right prior to the good. As per above, a disagreement upon issues of philosophical substance is redescribed as a case of what amounts to selfishness.

Consider specifically the case of the citizen of faith (A) who, we imagine, participates in the following dialogue with the keeper of the keys (B) to the Original Position.

A: So this is the place where we reason together and determine how to live by principles of justice? I'm all for that, and happy to be here.

B: Good. You know you'll have to leave your knowledge of matters irrelevant from the point of view of justice behind before you enter in here.

A: By all means, by all means! You know, we have a story that this place reminds me of a little bit. It's about the last being made first, and the lion lying down with the lamb. . . .

B: Yeah, yeah, well, there are no stories in here. Stories are particular. That's your story, not everybody's. You'll have to leave it behind to come in.

A: Well, I suppose, if you say so. Though my particular story is about universal things, you know.

B: It's a rule. But hey, it applies to everyone equally, so don't feel put out.

A: I see your point. Fair enough. So what shall I leave behind here?

B: Here, put it in this sack and you can pick it up on your way out. Race, gender, occupation, wealth. . . .

A: Yes, yes, if you could just help me a bit with this, it's a bit difficult to remove. But really, this is splendid. It must be like one big family in there.

B: Family? What family do you mean? There's lots of different kinds of families.

A: Yes, I'm sure there are. Well, never mind. Is that everything? I'm feeling rather thin, you know.

B: Almost everything. Put your conception of the good on top of the pile there.

A: I don't believe I have one, though I'm not sure. I never heard of a "conception of the good" before.

B: Look, don't hold out on me, friend; everybody's got one. We get a lot of folks trying to sneak through with their conception of the good. It says here on my register you're a Christian. Is that right?

A: I try to be.

B: Well, whatever. Look, you have to leave your Christianity here, too. That's your conception of the good.

A: But then how will I be able to talk about justice when I get in there?

B: Don't worry about it. You'll do fine. There are plenty of Christians walking around who talk about justice all the time without bringing religion into it.

A: Well, perhaps, but I'm afraid I'm not one of them. But isn't this the place where we're going to determine the most fundamental rules of political order?

B: Right. You go in and make up the rules. Then you come out and we give you your personal stuff back, at least all that's admissible within the rules.

A: You mean I don't necessarily get it all back?

B: Hey, look, what do you want, special treatment? You believe in justice, don't you?

A: Absolutely.

B: Well, do you think people ought to be allowed to do things that violate justice?

A: No, not at all.

B: Well there you go. Take your conception of the good, for example. If it's within the rules of justice, then they stamp it with a big machine that says "REASONABLE,"and you get it back. If not, it gets stamped "UNREASONABLE," and you have to talk with some counselors about some of the problems you might face when you leave.

A: Let me make sure I have this right. You want me to take off my Christianity, and then make up some rules, and then see whether my Christianity fits the rules or not before I put it back on? And if it doesn't fit the rules, I'm not supposed to put it back on?

B: Yeah, that's about it. Hey, look, what do you want? Everybody does the same. The boss says when we get Christians who don't like the idea, we should give them this book to read, to help them see things more clearly. Here, take a copy. [Hands him Kant's Religion within the Limits of Reason Alone]

A: [Taking the book] Oh, I'm afraid I prefer Kierkegaard. I just can't do it. I don't even know if I could get this Christianity off of me even if I wanted to.

B: Sure you could. Jeez, you sound like some of those feminists over there, who say they can't remove their gender.

A: Well, it doesn't matter. There's no way I'm taking it off.

B: Yeah? Well, I guess I had you figured wrong. I didn't take you for a guy who won't play by the rules unless he's sure he's going to win. You can line up over there, beside the rich folks hanging on to their money. You know what? They all have big, fine conceptions of the good, too, which they claim shows how they deserve what they have. Anyway, just go on over there. If you can't live on the basis of equality and respect for people different from you, you can't come in here.

A: I think there must be some misunderstanding. I believe in the equality of all people, and I certainly think we ought to try to respect people who are different from us.

B: Well, apparently you don't believe in it as much as you claim. If you did, you'd take off your religion. After all, what are you so worried about? If your religion is all you take it to be, you won't have any problems. Seems to me the fact you're afraid to take it off shows that you know it might not pass muster. Otherwise, you wouldn't be afraid.

A: I don't think you understand. I'm not afraid of anything, and I don't want anything for myself. But Christianity is *why* I believe in these things, and it is *how* I know about justice. When I saw your flyer about "people who want to live together in freedom and equality," I thought, boy, this is the place for a guy like me. Now I'm not so sure.

And one more thing. It's not "my" conception of the good, or "my" religion. It's not a personal possession of mine. I wish you'd quit referring to it like that.

B: [*Sighing*] Just a minute. [*Shouting off to the side*]: Hey, boss, we got another one of them fanatics here . . .

The difference here seems to me irreconcilable. The fundamental condition of entering the original position is a condition the citizen of faith cannot, in good conscience, accept. This difference will prevent any full-fledged reconciliation of the two points of view, even in cases where the substantive values at the heart of the citizen of faith's conception of political justice and those at the heart of the Rawlsian liberal's conception of justice are very similar. In refusing to enter the original position, the citizen of faith is trying to acknowledge the authority of God over him. But from the point of view of the original position, this citizen is being recalcitrant and failing to show equal respect for his fellows by insisting on viewing politics in light of the good (or, as the liberal would have it, in light of "his conception of" the good). The refusal to enter the original position is functionally analogous to the refusal to commit oneself to using only liberal public reasons when thinking about basic questions of justice. The citizen of faith, then, is left with the possibility of establishing a conditional agreement with the Rawlsian liberal about matters of basic justice. Presumably, from the Rawlsian point of view, this will amount to a *modus vivendi* rather than the achievement of a genuine overlapping consensus.

But there are other ways to think about the relation between the citizen of faith and Rawlsian liberalism. The sketch above treats the original position in a more or less literal fashion, and incorporates the idea of a linear sequence of steps in thinking about the relationship between political justice and conceptions of the good. There is another model for thinking about this in *A Theory of Justice*, and it is arguably much closer to expressing the full spirit of Rawls's thinking than is the idea sketched above. This other model is centered around the notion of reflective equilibrium. Here, we imagine the original position not as the foundation of all further talk about justice, but as one variable among others to be adjusted in light of reflection. In *A Theory of Justice*, Rawls speaks of our "considered convictions of justice" as one variable which is brought into play in the process of seeking reflective equilibrium.[21] Indeed, the equilibrium referred to is one between these considered convictions on the one hand, and the theory of justice and its attendant notions such as the description of the original position on the other. Speaking of how we are to adjust the definition of the original position in light of how its results look when seen in the light of our considered convictions, Rawls wrote:

> But presumably there will be discrepancies. In this case we have a choice. We can either modify the account of the initial situation or we can revise our existing judgments, for even the judgments we take provisionally as fixed points are liable to revision. By going back and forth, sometimes altering the conditions of the contractual circumstances, at others withdrawing our judgments and conforming them to principle, I assume that eventually we shall find a description of the initial situation that both expresses reasonable conditions and yields principles which match our considered judgments duly pruned and adjusted. This state of affairs I refer to as reflective equilibrium.[22]

I am not concerned with the details of Rawls' idea of reflective equilibrium but rather with the contrast between it and the foundationalist understanding of the original position sketched previously. On the reflective equilibrium model, there is room for understanding the sense in which a conscientiously motivated moral reasoner might reject the requirements of the original position (or, to put it more directly, the substantive philosophical and political ideas those requirements express) as understood by Rawls. Thus, the citizen of faith's "considered judgments" might be taken to include his religious understanding of the world. I do not mean to suggest that this is Rawls's intention; I suspect he would resist it. The use of phrases like "duly pruned and adjusted" displays an awareness of the potential that "our" considered convictions may not all be the same ones, and that to allow them the considerable degree of weight they bear in reflective equilibrium may threaten to undermine consensus on basic principles of justice. This possibility is submerged in the text beneath the constant invocation of "our" as the (presumably unified) subject of (a presumably single) set of considered convictions. That they are "duly pruned and adjusted" provides a further (unspecified) hedge against the possibility of things getting out of hand. Nevertheless, in spite of these factors, it is still the case that the idea of reflective equilibrium does acknowledge both the significance and the legitimacy of referring to one's *actual* ethical beliefs when it comes to evaluating theories of political justice. And that perspective provides a point of view from which the recalcitrance of the citizen of faith, when asked to give his wholehearted commitment to a Rawlsian account of justice, could readily be understood as something more than mere selfishness.

Moreover, the model of reflective equilibrium also provides a point of view which enables us to see that the Rawlsian liberal and the citizen of faith are in a much more similar position with regard to the relation between justice and comprehensive view than might first appear to be the case. The citizen of faith is, as it were, worried about whether or not the principles of Rawlsian justice run afoul of the commands of God. He treats those commands (or more precisely, his best understanding of those commands) as ultimately authoritative, and therefore will not agree to commit himself to the principle of employing only public reasons when making political judgments. The Rawlsian liberal stands in *what appears to be* a different relation to justice. He does not hesitate, as it were, to assent to the principles of political liberalism. He would appear to be unlike the recalcitrant citizen of faith, in not holding political justice hostage to the review of his own comprehensive view.

But this is an illusion. Rawls's discourse in *Political Liberalism* almost always proceeds against the background assumption of a society which to a substantial degree embodies widespread commitment to the fundamental principles of political liberalism. A very important consequence of this is that Rawls never addresses the following possible scenario: What if the principles of justice regulating the political realm in a society were to contradict the fundamental requirements of the comprehensive moral view which John Rawls holds? (This is the Rawlsian version of the question that troubles the citizen of faith.) This scenario never comes up because Rawls's discourse posits an account of political justice (political liberalism) which *by definition* is not incompatible with the comprehensive moral theory of liberalism (presumably the comprehensive Kantian liberalism of *A Theory of Justice*). Assuming such congruence, there can be no rupture between politics and morality. On the other hand, if the congruence is *not* assumed, then I suppose that Rawls, and any other comprehensive liberal, would respond in exactly the same fashion as I described the citizen of faith responding above. That is to say, confronted with the question of whether he would wholeheartedly affirm some principles of politics that claim to be just ones, I assume that Rawls and any other comprehensive liberal would reserve an answer until such principles were specified so that he or she could assess them in light of his or her comprehensive view and the considered convictions which are part and parcel of it.

Now I don't mean to be understood as criticizing Rawls for, in effect, *assuming* a congruence between his comprehensive moral view and the political view of justice he defends. This is perfectly ordinary, indeed so ordinary that it seems to me that *everyone* would do exactly the same, though of course the substantive content of their congruent views might differ.[23] That is to say, no one holds (or at least no one intentionally holds[24]) a view of normative[25] political principles that would yield duties contradictory to the duties prescribed by that same person's comprehensive moral view. This is one sense in which political views show themselves to be related to comprehensive moral views, and thus are not entirely freestanding. I do not say they are simple *repetitions* of the comprehensive views, and I accept the Rawlsian idea of a political view being such that it is open to being affirmed by more than one comprehensive view. The view I take here does deny, however, that the political can be understood as completely autonomous from the moral. I take Rawls to agree with that, though this is sometimes made unclear by his usage of the adjective "freestanding" to describe the view of the political he tries to work out (political liberalism). Speaking precisely, political liberalism can only be partially, not wholly, freestanding from the comprehensive views of liberalism. If it were wholly freestanding, congruence could not be assured.

Rawls's position is thus no different from anyone else's when it comes to testing a political view with reference to a comprehensive view, but this fact is often obscured because his textual discourse usually proceeds on the assumption that the society being discussed is founded on political principles that in his judgment are the best candidates for achieving justice. Thus Rawls (or the liberal generally) can appear to be (though he is not in fact) in a different relation to political justice than is the citizen of faith, who, upon the basis of his reason and reflection, rejects the constitutive ideas of Rawls's political liberalism. That citizen can appear to be one who refuses to accept and play by the rules of political justice. His vice appears to be that of selfishly insisting upon withholding assent to principles of political justice until he determines whether those principles will allow him to, as the Rawlsian liberal might put it, "advance his own conception of the good."

But this is quite misleading. Rawls's theory of justice as fairness specifically, and his idea of political liberalism generally, are *candidates* for occupying the theoretical space created by the general and abstract idea of "justice" simply. They cannot simply be equated with justice itself. Of course, they are not arbitrary candidates. Rawls explicates them at great length and with considerable sophistication and power, and in a sense this overall explication is itself the argument in support of them. Still, it is by no means obvious that Rawls's particular view of political justice is in fact the correct and true instantiation of the idea of justice. It is in competition with other ideas, ideas that are similarly the product of the reason and reflection of those intelligent and conscientious thinkers who advance, have advanced and presumably will continue to advance them.

There is another feature of Rawls's account that tends to submerge from view the potential tension between a liberal comprehensive view and the terms of political justice. This is Rawls's decision in *Political Liberalism* to treat political liberalism as a doctrine appropriate to the context of a "modern constitutional democracy" (sometimes called a "democratic regime" or "constitutional regime under modern conditions").[26] This leaves aside the questions of whether liberal principles of political justice might be true in a philosophical sense and/or applicable to persons and societies more universally. This move on Rawls's part has elicited much comment, most of it revolving around the issue of whether Rawls might have moved too far in the direction of communitarianism or a latent skepticism about truth.[27] But for our purpose, what is interesting about it is that it in effect posits certain very general values, such as liberty and equality, as constitutive components of the conception of justice under discussion in his texts. To the degree that these values are understood as liberal values,[28] this positing again functions to remove from the realm of possibility the chance of a deep conflict between a liberal comprehensive view and the demands of political justice. For upon the basis of this positing, we are in effect supposing for the sake of all further argument that the best account of justice will be a recognizably liberal account. The comprehensive liberal is thus assured of congruence between comprehensive morality and political justice. But, of course, the philosophical question of whether comprehensive liberal morality and the true account of political justice are compatible with one another is an open question. To the degree that we remember this, we can again see that the comprehensive liberal is no different from the citizen of faith when it comes to respecting the claims of political justice. Both will do so insofar as the specific account of justice under review passes the test of evaluation before their respective comprehensive views.

It might help to consider what the issue would look like if we reversed positions. Imagine that a comprehensive liberal is asked whether he can wholeheartedly affirm an account of political justice which, although developed from the perspective of a religious faith, is now being presented as "freestanding" in the hopes that even those who don't agree with that faith might nevertheless assent to its provisions and requirements. What could he say, other than "let me look at it and see what it amounts to in specifics and then I'll tell you whether I can go along with it or not." The religious citizen, in *this* example, does not evince a similar hesitation. Assured of congruence between comprehensive religious view and account of political justice, he affirms his respect for justice (as he sees it) immediately. And perhaps he notices the hesitation of his comprehensive liberal friend, and wonders at the depth of his commitment to justice. But this would be unfair, for his friend is as committed to living as justly as he is, though he may not agree about what this entails.

Conclusion

So we return to Rawls's question: Is it possible for citizens of faith who endorse society's intrinsic political ideals and values and do not simply acquiesce in the balance of political and social forces to be wholehearted members of a democratic society?[29] Is it possible for them to offer suitably "firm allegiance" to the well-ordered society of political liberalism, thus contributing to "stability for the right reasons"? Rawls thinks that they can, but I have suggested that the answer to the questions must remain indeterminate because of the lack of specificity in Rawls's text regarding the implications of "wholehearted" and "firm allegiance." The problem is that Rawls specifies what the "right reasons" are only indirectly and incompletely, by specifying what one set of wrong reasons is. Of course, some citizens of faith (like some other citizens without religious faith) will withhold anything other than prudential assent to political liberalism because they will reject outright the fundamental values which are constitutive of political liberalism. As Rawls says bluntly in "Public Reason Revisited," "political liberalism does not engage those who think this way."[30] But I have been concerned throughout with the citizen of faith who understands himself to be committed to the political values of liberty and equality, who does not think that the failure of his fellows to share his faith is to be understood as a sign of irrationality or unreasonability on their part, and who is understood to be a "liberal" in the ordinary sense of everyday politics. This citizen of faith, I have argued, is certainly capable of affirming the principles of political liberalism (should he decide in good conscience that they are the best of those available, where "best" means judged with knowledge and in light of his fundamental religious beliefs) in a sense stronger than merely the prudential one. But whether that stronger sense is sufficient to constitute "right reasons" from the Rawlsian point of view is unclear. For the citizen of faith, I have argued that it cannot in good conscience be made "strong" to the point that he accepts the priority of (what political liberalism defines as) purely political values over the demands of his comprehensive view. If the yardstick of "right reasons" is the granting of that priority, then my claim is that citizens of faith cannot, and indeed ought not, evince the commitment that political liberalism asks of them.

The fact that Rawls clearly hopes that political liberalism can and will attract the right kind of allegiance from most citizens of faith is one factor that might lead him to endorse the weak reading of "commitment for the right reasons." However, the fact that comprehensive liberals are portrayed as giving full assent to the priority of the political values of liberal public reason over their comprehensive liberalisms suggests that he takes such "strong" commitment to be necessary for stability for the right reasons. It is easy to lose sight of this fact when thinking about Rawls's arguments in *Political Liberalism* and "Public Reason Revisited" that speak directly to citizens of faith. When so speaking, Rawls is asking whether citizens of faith can *join* an overlapping consensus of other comprehensive views in support of political liberalism. There is, then, an overlapping consensus that, as it were, already exists, and one supposes that this must be comprised largely of comprehensive liberals of various sorts (Rawls often mentions Kantian and Millian versions of comprehensive liberalism). These citizens will have accepted the requirement of political liberalism that in making decisions about basic justice and constitutional essentials they employ the political values of liberal public reason and avoid appeal to terms of their comprehensive views that can be reasonably rejected by their fellow citizens. For them, there is a two-step process involved here. Their comprehensive views *do* come into play in providing them with reasons to affirm political liberalism (step 1). Given that affirmation, they then (step 2) commit to bracketing their comprehensive views and using only political values when thinking about the basic political questions.[31] This seems to me the paradigmatic structure in Rawls's text for commitment to political liberalism for the right reasons. If so, then (many) citizens of faith will conscientiously refuse to meet it. For I do not think they can accept the second step. This refusal should not be misinterpreted either as a selfish insistence on holding out for a better deal for one's personal interests, or as a refusal to show respect for one's fellow citizens as equals. It is a failure to show equal respect only if the best specific understanding of that general idea is the interpretation offered by Rawls in the form of his account of public reason and the duty of civility. But that interpretation is a highly contentious one. My own view is similar to that of William Galston, who argues that "we show others respect when we offer them, as explanation, what we take to be our true and best reasons for acting as we do."[32] If that is so, then a refusal to affirm the demands of public reason in the paradigmatic sense above is not a failure to show equal respect for one's fellows. Indeed, if Galston is right, then it is the demand itself that comes closer to qualifying as showing a lack of equal respect for one's fellows.

Nor should a refusal to assent to Rawls's account of public reason be misconstrued as a decision to treat politics as a marketplace of competing interests rather than a forum of principle. Again, that would be to assume that the general idea of democratic politics as a deliberative forum of principle is correctly captured and expressed by the specific interpretation of Rawlsian public reason. But that, too, is a highly contentious assumption. Many citizens who agree with the general idea that political power ought to be exercised in ways that are responsive to reflective thinking and respectful of the equal moral and political standing of their fellow citizens will nevertheless reject the specific interpretation of these general values offered by Rawls. These citizens may, of course, be wrong in so rejecting Rawls's interpretations, and a Rawlsian would presumably think them wrong for so doing. But as far as I can see, to call them unreasonable for such a rejection is an especially unfortunate misdescription. It is interesting to note in this respect the irony of the fact that Rawls's account of "reasonableness" in *Political Liberalism* has proven to be so controversial.[33] Rawls retreated from claims of truth to claims of reasonableness on behalf of political liberalism as part of an attempt to avoid alienating potential sources of support for it by removing issues of an intractable philosophical and religious character from the discussion of political justice. Arguably, however, one displays greater respect for one's adversaries by simply stating clearly that one thinks their views are wrong rather than avoiding the question of truth and describing their views as "unreasonable" (though, in theory, possibly true).

If the strong reading of Rawls's requirements for stability for the right reasons is correct, then citizens of faith will at best be able to establish something of a *modus vivendi* agreement with comprehensive liberals to abide by the Rawlsian account of political liberalism. This is not to say they would necessarily do so. That will depend, obviously, on the substantive content of their comprehensive religious and moral views, and also upon what the alternatives are.[34]

It is not at all clear that this would really be much of a loss from the point of view of the comprehensive liberal. Allowing that citizens of faith would be committed "more than prudentially, but less than wholeheartedly," there is no reason to think that a stable constitutional order would not result. It would not qualify as a "well-ordered" society from Rawls's perspective, but given the laxness of the latest version of Rawls's views of the requirements of public reason, it is plausible to think that he might not view this as a serious problem. Presumably, political liberals in power would have bigger problems to worry about than the fact that citizens of faith who were more or less liberal in their substantive political views would not, as it were, sign what amounts to a loyalty oath. Conversely, it might seem that it is somewhat churlish for such citizens of faith to make too much of the difference here. To put it more pointedly, and in terms related to the real world situation of liberalism as a political movement in the United States at the turn of the century, one might ask whether social democrats, secular liberals, and liberal Christians have bigger problems to deal with than quarreling with one another over the issue of commitment. I think the answer to that question, at least, is easy: They do.

Notes

1. There are three primary texts in this regard. (1) "Reply to Habermas" was a response to an essay by Jürgen Habermas, published in *Journal of Philosophy*, 92, no. 3 (March 1995), 132–80. This was republished in the paperback edition of *Political Liberalism*. New

York: Columbia University Press, 1996. This edition also contained (2) an important essay titled "Introduction to the paperback edition," pp. xxxvii–lxii. This introduction is close to but not identical with (3) "The Idea of Public Reason Revisited," *University of Chicago Law Review*, 64, no. 3 (summer, 1997), 765–807. The present essay concentrates upon the latter two texts. All references to *Political Liberalism* are to the paperback edition.

2. See his "Introduction: Religion and the Liberalism of Reasoned Respect," in *Religion and Contemporary Liberalism*, ed. Paul J. Weithman. Notre Dame, Ind.: University of Notre Dame Press, 1997, pp. 1–37.

3. Please note: ignoring the demands of the Rawlsian notion of the duty of civility is not to be confused with behaving uncivilly.

4. The term "citizen of faith" is Rawls's term, and I shall use it as well in this essay, in spite of the fact that it creates many perplexities and problems for analysis. "Citizen of faith" is a generic term, grouping into one category people who believe in and practice, as a matter of actual fact, not a generic thing designated "faith," but many different particular faiths. From the point of view of liberalism, the term "citizen of faith," like "religion," is a kind of umbrella concept that unites at one level of conceptualization phenomena that may be seen as different at another (I do not say lower). In this respect, "religion" is a concept not so much in tension with "liberalism" as it is one that, alongside whatever elements of tension may be thought to exist, is "already" prepared for a role within liberal discourse and theory. Or to put it more concretely, I hypothesize that liberal theory finds it easier to talk about the claims of "religion" on liberal principles than it does to talk about the claims of "Christianity" or "Judaism" on liberal principles. Theory-talk about "religion" is respectable. Theory-talk about "Christianity" or "Judaism" is permissible, but fraught with danger. But what danger? It seems to me the danger is that of *substantive particularity*. Consider John Howard Yoder's speculative remarks: "The search for a public moral language is motivated rather by embarrassment about particularity, which is not willing to break through the embarrassment to confession by taking the risk of specific encounter, preferring to posit something argued to be more solid and less threatening than an open market place, even if that 'something' be

nonexistent or vacuous." (John Howard Yoder, *The Priestly King-dom*. Notre Dame, Ind.: University of Notre Dame Press, 1984, p. 42)
My conception of a "citizen of faith" for this essay is doubtless colored in many ways by my own faith, that of a Protestant Christian, and the tendency, conscious and unconscious, to interpret the general category in light of that particular understanding.

5. Rawls, "Public Reason Revisited," pp. 779–80.

6. This lesson has been vigorously illustrated by Stanley Hauerwas. See, for example, *Resident Aliens: Life in the Christian Colony*. Nashville, Tenn.: Abingdon Press, 1989.

7. Allowing for this, the difference is nevertheless instructive in the context of Rawls's attempt to articulate the terms of an allegedly public reason. A term that is casually and mundanely used by him is anything but casual and mundane to me, given the perspective of a citizen of faith. The first thing I think of when considering whole-hearted commitment to a political regime is the crowing of a cock. (See Gospel of Mark 14:16–72.)

8. Rawls, "Public Reason Revisited," p. 780.

9. Ibid.

10. Ibid.

11. Ibid., p. 781.

12. Ibid.

13. Ibid.

14. A point stressed in relation to Rawls in Jeremy Waldron, "Disagreements About Justice," *Pacific Philosophical Quarterly*, 75, nos. 3–4 (fall 1994), 372–87.

15. Rawls, *Political Liberalism*, p. xxiv.

16. Ibid., pp. 54–58.

17. Rawls, "Public Reason Revisited," pp. 805–06.

18. Ibid., p. 804.

19. John Rawls, *A Theory of Justice*, Cambridge, Mass.: Harvard University Press, 1971, p. 18.

20. Ibid.

21. Ibid., p. 20.

22. Ibid.

23. When I say "assuming" here, I don't mean it in the sense of believing something without reflection or consideration. The term is not

meant pejoratively. Rather, I mean that, much as in Rawls's notion of reflective equilibrium, people will reflectively bring their views of political justice into line with their comprehensive views.

24. I ignore for present purposes the case of the person who is mistaken in believing his views to be congruent because they contain contradictory elements he does not see or understand. In so doing, I probably ignore what is in effect most of us, most of the time.

25. The insertion of "normative" here is to distinguish the present discussion from one in which "political" could be taken to denote a Machiavellian realm of conflict and intrigue that is defined as contrary to morality in its essence. I do not say the Machiavellian view is wrong, only that we are ignoring it for present purposes.

26. Rawls, *Political Liberalism*, p. 11.

27. See esp. Joseph Raz, "Facing Diversity: The Case of Epistemic Abstinence," *Philosophy and Public Affairs*, 19, no. 3 (1990), pp. 3–52, and Jean Hampton, "Should Political Philosophy Be Done Without Metaphysics?" *Ethics*, 99, no. 4 (1989), pp. 791–815.

28. The careful phrasing is intentional. Liberals believe in liberty and equality, but liberty and equality are not simply liberal values. One can believe in liberty and equality without being a liberal. Liberty and equality are not the private property of liberals.

29. The phrase in Rawls's question makes no mention of the society being based on the principles of political liberalism, but the context makes it clear that Rawls is referring not simply to a "democratic society" generally, but rather to a democratic society ordered according to the principles of political liberalism.

30. Rawls, "Public Reason Revisited," p. 767.

31. Ibid., p. 777.

32. William Galston, *Liberal Purposes: Goods, Virtue and Diversity in the Liberal State*. Cambridge, UK: Cambridge University Press, 1991, p. 109.

33. An especially tart critique is Paul Campos, "Secular Fundamentalism," *Columbia Law Review*, 94, no. 6 (October 1994), pp. 1814–27.

34. For example, I'd sign on to the difference principle, but would prefer a less antiperfectionist approach to liberty than the Rawlsian one.

Contributors

JOHN FINNIS, Professor of Law and Legal Philosophy, Oxford University; Biolchini Professor of Law, University of Notre Dame. He is the author of *Natural Law and Natural Rights* (1980).

ROBERT P. GEORGE, Cyrus McCormick Professor of Jurisprudence, Department of Politics, Princeton University. He is the author of *In Defense of Natural Law* (1999).

STEPHEN MACEDO, Laurance Rockefeller Professor, Center for Human Values, Princeton University. He is the author of *Liberal Virtues* (1990).

PATRICK NEAL, Professor, Department of Political Science, University of Vermont. He is the author of *Liberalism and Its Discontents* (1997).

JEFFREY REIMAN, William Fraser McDowell Professor of Philosophy, American University, Washington, DC. He is the author of *Critical Moral Liberalism* (1997).

PAUL J. WEITHMAN, Associate Professor, Department of Philosophy, University of Notre Dame. He is the author of *Religion and Contemporary Liberalism* (1997).

CHRISTOPHER WOLFE, Professor and Chairman, Department of Political Science, Marquette University, and President of the American Philosophy Institute. He is the author of *The Rise of Modern Judicial Review* (1986).

Index

Page references followed by "n." or "nn." refer to information in notes.